Syllabus

SUPREME COURT OF THE UNITED STATES

Syllabus

CITIZENS UNITED *v.* FEDERAL ELECTION COMMISSION

APPEAL FROM THE UNITED STATES DISTRICT COURT FOR THE DISTRICT OF COLUMBIA

No. 08–205.   Argued March 24, 2009—Reargued September 9, 2009—
Decided January 21, 2010

As amended by §203 of the Bipartisan Campaign Reform Act of 2002 (BCRA), federal law prohibits corporations and unions from using their general treasury funds to make independent expenditures for speech that is an "electioneering communication" or for speech that expressly advocates the election or defeat of a candidate. 2 U. S. C. §441b. An electioneering communication is "any broadcast, cable, or satellite communication" that "refers to a clearly identified candidate for Federal office" and is made within 30 days of a primary election, §434(f)(3)(A), and that is "publicly distributed," 11 CFR §100.29(a)(2), which in "the case of a candidate for nomination for President . . . means" that the communication "[c]an be received by 50,000 or more persons in a State where a primary election . . . is being held within 30 days," §100.29(b)(3)(ii). Corporations and unions may establish a political action committee (PAC) for express advocacy or electioneering communications purposes. 2 U. S. C. §441b(b)(2). In *McConnell* v. *Federal Election Comm'n*, 540 U. S. 93, 203–209, this Court upheld limits on electioneering communications in a facial challenge, relying on the holding in *Austin* v. *Michigan Chamber of Commerce*, 494 U. S. 652, that political speech may be banned based on the speaker's corporate identity.

In January 2008, appellant Citizens United, a nonprofit corporation, released a documentary (hereinafter *Hillary*) critical of then-Senator Hillary Clinton, a candidate for her party's Presidential nomination. Anticipating that it would make *Hillary* available on cable television through video-on-demand within 30 days of primary elections, Citizens United produced television ads to run on broadcast and cable television. Concerned about possible civil and criminal penalties for violating §441b, it sought declaratory and injunctive relief, arguing that (1) §441b is unconstitutional as applied to *Hillary;* and (2) BCRA's disclaimer, disclosure, and reporting requirements, BCRA §§201 and 311, were unconstitutional as applied to *Hillary* and the ads. The District Court denied Citizens United a preliminary injunction and granted appellee Federal Election Commission (FEC) summary judgment.

Held:

   1. Because the question whether §441b applies to *Hillary* cannot be resolved on other, narrower grounds without chilling political speech, this Court must consider the continuing effect of the speech suppression upheld in *Austin.* Pp. 5–20.

   (a) Citizen United's narrower arguments—that *Hillary* is not an "electioneering communication" covered by §441b because it is not "publicly distributed" under 11 CFR §100.29(a)(2); that §441b may not be applied to *Hillary* under *Federal Election Comm'n* v. *Wisconsin Right to Life, Inc.*, 551 U. S. 449 *(WRTL),* which found §441b unconstitutional as applied to speech that was not "express advocacy or its functional equivalent," *id.,* at 481 (opinion of ROBERTS, C. J.), determining that a communication "is the functional equivalent of express advocacy only if [it] is susceptible of no reasonable interpretation other than as an appeal to vote for or against a specific candidate," *id.,* at 469–470; that §441b should be invalidated as applied to movies shown through video-on-demand because this delivery system has a lower risk of distorting the political process than do television ads; and that there should be an exception to §441b's ban for nonprofit corporate political speech funded overwhelming by individuals—are not sustainable under a fair reading of the statute. Pp. 5–12.

   (b) Thus, this case cannot be resolved on a narrower ground without chilling political speech, speech that is central to the First Amendment's meaning and purpose. Citizens United did not waive this challenge to *Austin* when it stipulated to dismissing the facial challenge below, since (1) even if such a challenge could be waived, this Court may reconsider *Austin* and §441b's facial validity here because the District Court "passed upon" the issue, *Lebron* v. *National Railroad Passenger Corporation,* 513 U. S. 374, 379; (2) throughout the litigation, Citizens United has asserted a claim that the FEC has violated its right to free speech; and (3) the parties cannot enter into a stipulation that prevents the Court from considering remedies necessary to resolve a claim that has been preserved. Because Citizen United's narrower arguments are not sustainable, this Court must, in an exercise of its judicial responsibility, consider §441b's facial validity. Any other course would prolong the substantial, nationwide chilling effect caused by §441b's corporate expenditure ban. This conclusion is further supported by the following: (1) the uncertainty caused by the Government's litigating position; (2) substantial time would be required to clarify §441b's application on the points raised by the Government's position in order to avoid any chilling effect caused by an improper interpretation; and (3) because speech itself is of primary importance to the integrity of the election process, any speech arguably within the reach of rules created for regulating political speech is chilled. The regulatory scheme at issue may not be a prior restraint in the strict sense. However, given its complexity and the deference courts show to administrative determinations, a speaker wishing to avoid criminal liability threats and the heavy costs of defending against FEC enforcement must ask a governmental agency for prior permission to speak. The restrictions thus function as the equivalent of a prior restraint, giving the FEC power analogous to the type of government practices that the First Amendment was drawn to prohibit. The ongoing chill on speech makes it necessary to invoke the earlier precedents that a statute that chills speech can and must be invalidated where its facial invalidity has been demonstrated. Pp. 12–20.

   2. *Austin* is overruled, and thus provides no basis for allowing the Government to limit corporate independent expenditures. Hence, §441b's restrictions on such expenditures are invalid and cannot be applied to *Hillary.* Given this conclusion, the part of *McConnell* that upheld BCRA §203's extension of §441b's restrictions on independent corporate expenditures is also overruled. Pp. 20–51.

   (a) Although the First Amendment provides that "Congress shall make no law . . . abridging the freedom of speech," §441b's prohibition on corporate independent expenditures is an outright ban on speech, backed by criminal sanctions. It is a ban notwithstanding the fact that a PAC created by a corporation can still speak, for a PAC is a separate association from the corporation. Because speech is an essential mechanism of democracy—it is the means to hold officials accountable to the people—political speech must prevail against laws that would suppress it by design or inadvertence. Laws burdening such speech are subject to strict scrutiny, which requires the Government to prove that the restriction "furthers a compelling interest and is narrowly tailored to achieve that interest." *WRTL,* 551 U. S., at 464. This language provides a sufficient framework for protecting the interests in this case. Premised on mistrust of governmental power, the First Amendment stands against attempts to disfavor certain subjects or viewpoints or to distinguish among different speakers, which may be a means to control content. The Government may also commit a constitutional wrong when by law it identifies certain preferred speakers. There is no basis for the proposition that, in the political speech context, the Government may impose restrictions on certain disfavored speakers. Both history and logic lead to this conclusion. Pp. 20–25.

(b) The Court has recognized that the First Amendment applies to corporations, *e.g., First Nat. Bank of Boston* v. *Bellotti,* 435 U. S. 765, 778, n. 14, and extended this protection to the context of political speech, see, *e.g., NAACP* v. *Button,* 371 U. S. 415, 428–429. Addressing challenges to the Federal Election Campaign Act of 1971, the *Buckley* Court upheld limits on direct contributions to candidates, 18 U. S. C. §608(b), recognizing a governmental interest in preventing *quid pro quo* corruption. 424 U. S., at 25–26. However, the Court invalidated §608(e)'s expenditure ban, which applied to individuals, corporations, and unions, because it "fail[ed] to serve any substantial governmental interest in stemming the reality or appearance of corruption in the electoral process," *id.,* at 47–48. While *Buckley* did not consider a separate ban on corporate and union independent expenditures found in §610, had that provision been challenged in *Buckley*'s wake, it could not have been squared with the precedent's reasoning and analysis. The *Buckley* Court did not invoke the overbreadth doctrine to suggest that §608(e)'s expenditure ban would have been constitutional had it applied to corporations and unions but not individuals. Notwithstanding this precedent, Congress soon recodified §610's corporate and union expenditure ban at 2 U. S. C. §441b, the provision at issue. Less than two years after *Buckley, Bellotti* reaffirmed the First Amendment principle that the Government lacks the power to restrict political speech based on the speaker's corporate identity. 435 U.S., at 784–785. Thus the law stood until *Austin* upheld a corporate independent expenditure restriction, bypassing *Buckley* and *Bellotti* by recognizing a new governmental interest in preventing "the corrosive and distorting effects of immense aggregations of [corporate] wealth . . . that have little or no correlation to the public's support for the corporation's political ideas." 494 U. S., at 660. Pp. 25–32.

(c) This Court is confronted with conflicting lines of precedent: a pre-*Austin* line forbidding speech restrictions based on the speaker's corporate identity and a post-*Austin* line permitting them. Neither *Austin*'s antidistortion rationale nor the Government's other justifications support §441b's restrictions. Pp. 32–47.

(1) The First Amendment prohibits Congress from fining or jailing citizens, or associations of citizens, for engaging in political speech, but *Austin*'s antidistortion rationale would permit the Government to ban political speech because the speaker is an association with a corporate form. Political speech is "indispensable to decision-

making in a democracy, and this is no less true because the speech comes from a corporation." *Bellotti, supra,* at 777 (footnote omitted). This protection is inconsistent with *Austin*'s rationale, which is meant to prevent corporations from obtaining " 'an unfair advantage in the political marketplace' " by using " 'resources amassed in the economic marketplace.' " 494 U. S., at 659. First Amendment protections do not depend on the speaker's "financial ability to engage in public discussion." *Buckley, supra,* at 49. These conclusions were reaffirmed when the Court invalidated a BCRA provision that increased the cap on contributions to one candidate if the opponent made certain expenditures from personal funds. *Davis* v. *Federal Election Comm'n,* 554 U. S. ___, ___. Distinguishing wealthy individuals from corporations based on the latter's special advantages of, *e.g.,* limited liability, does not suffice to allow laws prohibiting speech. It is irrelevant for First Amendment purposes that corporate funds may "have little or no correlation to the public's support for the corporation's political ideas." *Austin, supra,* at 660. All speakers, including individuals and the media, use money amassed from the economic marketplace to fund their speech, and the First Amendment protects the resulting speech. Under the antidistortion rationale, Congress could also ban political speech of media corporations. Although currently exempt from §441b, they accumulate wealth with the help of their corporate form, may have aggregations of wealth, and may express views "hav[ing] little or no correlation to the public's support" for those views. Differential treatment of media corporations and other corporations cannot be squared with the First Amendment, and there is no support for the view that the Amendment's original meaning would permit suppressing media corporations' political speech. *Austin* interferes with the "open marketplace" of ideas protected by the First Amendment. *New York State Bd. of Elections* v. *Lopez Torres,* 552 U. S. 196, 208. Its censorship is vast in its reach, suppressing the speech of both for-profit and nonprofit, both small and large, corporations. Pp. 32–40.

(2) This reasoning also shows the invalidity of the Government's other arguments. It reasons that corporate political speech can be banned to prevent corruption or its appearance. The *Buckley* Court found this rationale "sufficiently important" to allow contribution limits but refused to extend that reasoning to expenditure limits, 424 U. S., at 25, and the Court does not do so here. While a single *Bellotti* footnote purported to leave the question open, 435 U. S., at 788, n. 26, this Court now concludes that independent expenditures, including those made by corporations, do not give rise to corruption or the appearance of corruption. That speakers may have influence over or access to elected officials does not mean that those officials

are corrupt. And the appearance of influence or access will not cause the electorate to lose faith in this democracy. *Caperton* v. *A. T. Massey Coal Co.*, 556 U. S. ___, distinguished. Pp. 40–45.

(3) The Government's asserted interest in protecting shareholders from being compelled to fund corporate speech, like the anti-distortion rationale, would allow the Government to ban political speech even of media corporations. The statute is underinclusive; it only protects a dissenting shareholder's interests in certain media for 30 or 60 days before an election when such interests would be implicated in any media at any time. It is also overinclusive because it covers all corporations, including those with one shareholder. P. 46.

(4) Because §441b is not limited to corporations or associations created in foreign countries or funded predominantly by foreign shareholders, it would be overbroad even if the Court were to recognize a compelling governmental interest in limiting foreign influence over the Nation's political process. Pp. 46–47.

(d) The relevant factors in deciding whether to adhere to *stare decisis,* beyond workability—the precedent's antiquity, the reliance interests at stake, and whether the decision was well reasoned—counsel in favor of abandoning *Austin,* which itself contravened the precedents of *Buckley* and *Bellotti.* As already explained, *Austin* was not well reasoned. It is also undermined by experience since its announcement. Political speech is so ingrained in this country's culture that speakers find ways around campaign finance laws. Rapid changes in technology—and the creative dynamic inherent in the concept of free expression—counsel against upholding a law that restricts political speech in certain media or by certain speakers. In addition, no serious reliance issues are at stake. Thus, due consideration leads to the conclusion that *Austin* should be overruled. The Court returns to the principle established in *Buckley* and *Bellotti* that the Government may not suppress political speech based on the speaker's corporate identity. No sufficient governmental interest justifies limits on the political speech of nonprofit or for-profit corporations. Pp. 47–50.

3. BCRA §§201 and 311 are valid as applied to the ads for *Hillary* and to the movie itself. Pp. 50–57.

(a) Disclaimer and disclosure requirements may burden the ability to speak, but they "impose no ceiling on campaign-related activities," *Buckley,* 424 U. S., at 64, or "'"prevent anyone from speaking,"'" *McConnell, supra,* at 201. The *Buckley* Court explained that disclosure can be justified by a governmental interest in providing "the electorate with information" about election-related spending sources. The *McConnell* Court applied this interest in rejecting facial challenges to §§201 and 311. 540 U. S., at 196. However, the Court

Syllabus

acknowledged that as-applied challenges would be available if a group could show a "'reasonable probability'" that disclosing its contributors' names would "'subject them to threats, harassment, or reprisals from either Government officials or private parties.'" *Id.,* at 198. Pp. 50–52.

(b) The disclaimer and disclosure requirements are valid as applied to Citizens United's ads. They fall within BCRA's "electioneering communication" definition: They referred to then-Senator Clinton by name shortly before a primary and contained pejorative references to her candidacy. Section 311 disclaimers provide information to the electorate, *McConnell, supra,* at 196, and "insure that the voters are fully informed" about who is speaking, *Buckley, supra,* at 76. At the very least, they avoid confusion by making clear that the ads are not funded by a candidate or political party. Citizens United's arguments that §311 is underinclusive because it requires disclaimers for broadcast advertisements but not for print or Internet advertising and that §311 decreases the quantity and effectiveness of the group's speech were rejected in *McConnell.* This Court also rejects their contention that §201's disclosure requirements must be confined to speech that is the functional equivalent of express advocacy under *WRTL*'s test for restrictions on independent expenditures, 551 U. S., at 469–476 (opinion of ROBERTS, C.J.). Disclosure is the less-restrictive alternative to more comprehensive speech regulations. Such requirements have been upheld in *Buckley* and *McConnell.* Citizens United's argument that no informational interest justifies applying §201 to its ads is similar to the argument this Court rejected with regard to disclaimers. Citizens United finally claims that disclosure requirements can chill donations by exposing donors to retaliation, but offers no evidence that its members face the type of threats, harassment, or reprisals that might make §201 unconstitutional as applied. Pp. 52–55.

(c) For these same reasons, this Court affirms the application of the §§201 and 311 disclaimer and disclosure requirements to *Hillary.* Pp. 55–56.

Reversed in part, affirmed in part, and remanded.

KENNEDY, J., delivered the opinion of the Court, in which ROBERTS, C. J., and SCALIA and ALITO, JJ., joined, in which THOMAS, J., joined as to all but Part IV, and in which STEVENS, GINSBURG, BREYER, and SO-TOMAYOR, JJ., joined as to Part IV. ROBERTS, C. J., filed a concurring opinion, in which ALITO, J., joined. SCALIA, J., filed a concurring opinion, in which ALITO, J., joined, and in which THOMAS, J., joined in part. STEVENS, J., filed an opinion concurring in part and dissenting in part, in which GINSBURG, BREYER, and SOTOMAYOR, JJ., joined. THOMAS, J., filed an opinion concurring in part and dissenting in part.

NOTICE: This opinion is subject to formal revision before publication in the preliminary print of the United States Reports. Readers are requested to notify the Reporter of Decisions, Supreme Court of the United States, Washington, D. C. 20543, of any typographical or other formal errors, in order that corrections may be made before the preliminary print goes to press.

SUPREME COURT OF THE UNITED STATES

No. 08–205

CITIZENS UNITED, APPELLANT *v.* FEDERAL ELECTION COMMISSION

ON APPEAL FROM THE UNITED STATES DISTRICT COURT FOR THE DISTRICT OF COLUMBIA

[January 21, 2010]

JUSTICE KENNEDY delivered the opinion of the Court.

Federal law prohibits corporations and unions from using their general treasury funds to make independent expenditures for speech defined as an "electioneering communication" or for speech expressly advocating the election or defeat of a candidate. 2 U. S. C. §441b. Limits on electioneering communications were upheld in *McConnell* v. *Federal Election Comm'n*, 540 U. S. 93, 203–209 (2003). The holding of *McConnell* rested to a large extent on an earlier case, *Austin* v. *Michigan Chamber of Commerce*, 494 U. S. 652 (1990). *Austin* had held that political speech may be banned based on the speaker's corporate identity.

In this case we are asked to reconsider *Austin* and, in effect, *McConnell*. It has been noted that "*Austin* was a significant departure from ancient First Amendment principles," *Federal Election Comm'n* v. *Wisconsin Right to Life, Inc.*, 551 U. S. 449, 490 (2007) *(WRTL)* (SCALIA, J., concurring in part and concurring in judgment). We agree with that conclusion and hold that *stare decisis* does not compel the continued acceptance of *Austin*. The Govern-

ment may regulate corporate political speech through
disclaimer and disclosure requirements, but it may not
suppress that speech altogether. We turn to the case now
before us.

I

A

Citizens United is a nonprofit corporation. It brought
this action in the United States District Court for the
District of Columbia. A three-judge court later convened
to hear the cause. The resulting judgment gives rise to
this appeal.

Citizens United has an annual budget of about $12
million. Most of its funds are from donations by individuals; but, in addition, it accepts a small portion of its funds
from for-profit corporations.

In January 2008, Citizens United released a film entitled *Hillary: The Movie.* We refer to the film as *Hillary.* It
is a 90-minute documentary about then-Senator Hillary
Clinton, who was a candidate in the Democratic Party's
2008 Presidential primary elections. *Hillary* mentions
Senator Clinton by name and depicts interviews with
political commentators and other persons, most of them
quite critical of Senator Clinton. *Hillary* was released in
theaters and on DVD, but Citizens United wanted to
increase distribution by making it available through video-
on-demand.

Video-on-demand allows digital cable subscribers to
select programming from various menus, including movies, television shows, sports, news, and music. The viewer
can watch the program at any time and can elect to re-
wind or pause the program. In December 2007, a cable
company offered, for a payment of $1.2 million, to make
Hillary available on a video-on-demand channel called
"Elections '08." App. 255a–257a. Some video-on-demand
services require viewers to pay a small fee to view a se-

lected program, but here the proposal was to make *Hillary* available to viewers free of charge.

To implement the proposal, Citizens United was prepared to pay for the video-on-demand; and to promote the film, it produced two 10-second ads and one 30-second ad for *Hillary*. Each ad includes a short (and, in our view, pejorative) statement about Senator Clinton, followed by the name of the movie and the movie's Website address. *Id.*, at 26a–27a. Citizens United desired to promote the video-on-demand offering by running advertisements on broadcast and cable television.

B

Before the Bipartisan Campaign Reform Act of 2002 (BCRA), federal law prohibited—and still does prohibit—corporations and unions from using general treasury funds to make direct contributions to candidates or independent expenditures that expressly advocate the election or defeat of a candidate, through any form of media, in connection with certain qualified federal elections. 2 U. S. C. §441b (2000 ed.); see *McConnell, supra,* at 204, and n. 87; *Federal Election Comm'n* v. *Massachusetts Citizens for Life, Inc.,* 479 U. S. 238, 249 (1986) *(MCFL).* BCRA §203 amended §441b to prohibit any "electioneering communication" as well. 2 U. S. C. §441b(b)(2) (2006 ed.). An electioneering communication is defined as "any broadcast, cable, or satellite communication" that "refers to a clearly identified candidate for Federal office" and is made within 30 days of a primary or 60 days of a general election. §434(f)(3)(A). The Federal Election Commission's (FEC) regulations further define an electioneering communication as a communication that is "publicly distributed." 11 CFR §100.29(a)(2) (2009). "In the case of a candidate for nomination for President . . . *publicly distributed* means*" that the communication "[c]an be received by 50,000 or more persons in a State where a primary election . . . is being held within 30 days." §100.29(b)(3)(ii). Corporations and unions are barred from using their general treasury funds for express advocacy or electioneering communications. They may establish, however, a "separate segregated fund" (known as a political action committee, or PAC) for these purposes. 2 U. S. C. §441b(b)(2). The moneys received by the segregated fund are limited to donations from stockholders and employees of the corporation or, in the case of unions, members of the union. *Ibid.*

C

Citizens United wanted to make *Hillary* available through video-on-demand within 30 days of the 2008 primary elections. It feared, however, that both the film and the ads would be covered by §441b's ban on corporate-funded independent expenditures, thus subjecting the corporation to civil and criminal penalties under §437g. In December 2007, Citizens United sought declaratory and injunctive relief against the FEC. It argued that (1) §441b is unconstitutional as applied to *Hillary;* and (2) BCRA's disclaimer and disclosure requirements, BCRA §§201 and 311, are unconstitutional as applied to *Hillary* and to the three ads for the movie.

The District Court denied Citizens United's motion for a preliminary injunction, 530 F. Supp. 2d 274 (DC 2008) *(per curiam)*, and then granted the FEC's motion for summary judgment, App. 261a–262a. See *id.,* at 261a ("Based on the reasoning of our prior opinion, we find that the [FEC] is entitled to judgment as a matter of law. *See Citizen[s] United v. FEC,* 530 F. Supp. 2d 274 (D.D.C. 2008) (denying Citizens United's request for a preliminary injunction)"). The court held that §441b was facially constitutional under *McConnell,* and that §441b was constitutional as applied to *Hillary* because it was "susceptible of no other interpretation than to inform the electorate that Senator Clinton is unfit for office, that the United States would be a dangerous place in a President Hillary Clinton world, and that viewers should vote against her." 530 F. Supp. 2d, at 279. The court also rejected Citizens United's challenge to BCRA's disclaimer and disclosure requirements. It noted that "the Supreme Court has written approvingly of disclosure provisions triggered by political speech even though the speech itself was constitutionally protected under the First Amendment." *Id.*, at 281.

We noted probable jurisdiction. 555 U. S. ___ (2008). The case was reargued in this Court after the Court asked the parties to file supplemental briefs addressing whether we should overrule either or both *Austin* and the part of *McConnell* which addresses the facial validity of 2 U. S. C. §441b. See 557 U. S. ___ (2009).

II

Before considering whether *Austin* should be overruled, we first address whether Citizens United's claim that §441b cannot be applied to *Hillary* may be resolved on other, narrower grounds.

A

Citizens United contends that §441b does not cover *Hillary*, as a matter of statutory interpretation, because the film does not qualify as an "electioneering communication." §441b(b)(2). Citizens United raises this issue for the first time before us, but we consider the issue because "it was addressed by the court below." *Lebron* v. *National Railroad Passenger Corporation*, 513 U. S. 374, 379 (1995); see 530 F. Supp. 2d, at 277, n. 6. Under the definition of electioneering communication, the video-on-demand showing of *Hillary* on cable television would have been a "cable . . . communication" that "refer[red] to a clearly identified candidate for Federal office" and that was made within 30 days of a primary election. 2 U. S. C. §434(f)(3)(A)(i). Citizens United, however, argues that *Hillary* was not "publicly distributed," because a single video-on-demand transmission is sent only to a requesting cable converter box and each separate transmission, in most instances, will be seen by just one household—not 50,000 or more persons. 11 CFR §100.29(a)(2); see §100.29(b)(3)(ii).

This argument ignores the regulation's instruction on how to determine whether a cable transmission "[c]an be received by 50,000 or more persons." §100.29(b)(3)(ii). The regulation provides that the number of people who can receive a cable transmission is determined by the number of cable subscribers in the relevant area. §§100.29(b)(7)(i)(G), (ii). Here, Citizens United wanted to use a cable video-on-demand system that had 34.5 million subscribers nationwide. App. 256a. Thus, *Hillary* could have been received by 50,000 persons or more.

One *amici* brief asks us, alternatively, to construe the condition that the communication "[c]an be received by 50,000 or more persons," §100.29(b)(3)(ii)(A), to require "a plausible likelihood that the communication will be viewed by 50,000 or more potential voters"—as opposed to requiring only that the communication is "technologically capable" of being seen by that many people, Brief for Former Officials of the American Civil Liberties Union as *Amici Curiae* 5. Whether the population and demographic statistics in a proposed viewing area consisted of 50,000 registered voters—but not "infants, pre-teens, or otherwise electorally ineligible recipients"—would be a required determination, subject to judicial challenge and review, in any case where the issue was in doubt. *Id.*, at 6.

In our view the statute cannot be saved by limiting the reach of 2 U. S. C. §441b through this suggested interpretation. In addition to the costs and burdens of litigation, this result would require a calculation as to the number of people a particular communication is likely to reach, with

an inaccurate estimate potentially subjecting the speaker
to criminal sanctions. The First Amendment does not
permit laws that force speakers to retain a campaign
finance attorney, conduct demographic marketing research, or seek declaratory rulings before discussing the
most salient political issues of our day. Prolix laws chill
speech for the same reason that vague laws chill speech:
People "of common intelligence must necessarily guess at
[the law's] meaning and differ as to its application." *Con-
nally* v. *General Constr. Co.*, 269 U. S. 385, 391 (1926).
The Government may not render a ban on political speech
constitutional by carving out a limited exemption through
an amorphous regulatory interpretation. We must reject
the approach suggested by the *amici*. Section 441b covers
Hillary.

B

Citizens United next argues that §441b may not be
applied to *Hillary* under the approach taken in *WRTL*.
McConnell decided that §441b(b)(2)'s definition of an
"electioneering communication" was facially constitutional
insofar as it restricted speech that was "the functional
equivalent of express advocacy" for or against a specific
candidate. 540 U. S., at 206. *WRTL* then found an unconstitutional application of §441b where the speech was not
"express advocacy or its functional equivalent." 551 U. S.,
at 481 (opinion of ROBERTS, C. J.). As explained by THE
CHIEF JUSTICE's controlling opinion in *WRTL*, the func-
tional-equivalent test is objective: "a court should find that
[a communication] is the functional equivalent of express
advocacy only if [it] is susceptible of no reasonable interpretation other than as an appeal to vote for or against a
specific candidate." *Id.*, at 469–470.

Under this test, *Hillary* is equivalent to express advocacy. The movie, in essence, is a feature-length negative
advertisement that urges viewers to vote against Senator

Clinton for President. In light of historical footage, interviews with persons critical of her, and voiceover narration, the film would be understood by most viewers as an extended criticism of Senator Clinton's character and her fitness for the office of the Presidency. The narrative may contain more suggestions and arguments than facts, but there is little doubt that the thesis of the film is that she is unfit for the Presidency. The movie concentrates on alleged wrongdoing during the Clinton administration, Senator Clinton's qualifications and fitness for office, and policies the commentators predict she would pursue if elected President. It calls Senator Clinton "Machiavellian," App. 64a, and asks whether she is "the most qualified to hit the ground running if elected President," *id.*, at 88a. The narrator reminds viewers that "Americans have never been keen on dynasties" and that "a vote for Hillary is a vote to continue 20 years of a Bush or a Clinton in the White House," *id.*, at 143a–144a.

Citizens United argues that *Hillary* is just "a documentary film that examines certain historical events." Brief for Appellant 35. We disagree. The movie's consistent emphasis is on the relevance of these events to Senator Clinton's candidacy for President. The narrator begins by asking "could [Senator Clinton] become the first female President in the history of the United States?" App. 35a. And the narrator reiterates the movie's message in his closing line: "Finally, before America decides on our next president, voters should need no reminders of . . . what's at stake—the well being and prosperity of our nation." *Id.*, at 144a–145a.

As the District Court found, there is no reasonable interpretation of *Hillary* other than as an appeal to vote against Senator Clinton. Under the standard stated in *McConnell* and further elaborated in *WRTL*, the film qualifies as the functional equivalent of express advocacy.

C

Citizens United further contends that §441b should be invalidated as applied to movies shown through video-on-demand, arguing that this delivery system has a lower risk of distorting the political process than do television ads. Cf. *McConnell, supra,* at 207. On what we might call conventional television, advertising spots reach viewers who have chosen a channel or a program for reasons unrelated to the advertising. With video-on-demand, by contrast, the viewer selects a program after taking "a series of affirmative steps": subscribing to cable; navigating through various menus; and selecting the program. See *Reno* v. *American Civil Liberties Union,* 521 U. S. 844, 867 (1997).

While some means of communication may be less effective than others at influencing the public in different contexts, any effort by the Judiciary to decide which means of communications are to be preferred for the particular type of message and speaker would raise questions as to the courts' own lawful authority. Substantial questions would arise if courts were to begin saying what means of speech should be preferred or disfavored. And in all events, those differentiations might soon prove to be irrelevant or outdated by technologies that are in rapid flux. See *Turner Broadcasting System, Inc.* v. *FCC,* 512 U. S. 622, 639 (1994).

Courts, too, are bound by the First Amendment. We must decline to draw, and then redraw, constitutional lines based on the particular media or technology used to disseminate political speech from a particular speaker. It must be noted, moreover, that this undertaking would require substantial litigation over an extended time, all to interpret a law that beyond doubt discloses serious First Amendment flaws. The interpretive process itself would create an inevitable, pervasive, and serious risk of chilling protected speech pending the drawing of fine distinctions that, in the end, would themselves be questionable. First Amendment standards, however, "must give the benefit of any doubt to protecting rather than stifling speech." *WRTL*, 551 U. S., at 469 (opinion of ROBERTS, C. J.) (citing *New York Times Co.* v. *Sullivan*, 376 U. S. 254, 269–270 (1964)).

D

Citizens United also asks us to carve out an exception to §441b's expenditure ban for nonprofit corporate political speech funded overwhelmingly by individuals. As an alternative to reconsidering *Austin*, the Government also seems to prefer this approach. This line of analysis, however, would be unavailing.

In *MCFL*, the Court found unconstitutional §441b's restrictions on corporate expenditures as applied to nonprofit corporations that were formed for the sole purpose of promoting political ideas, did not engage in business activities, and did not accept contributions from for-profit corporations or labor unions. 479 U. S., at 263–264; see also 11 CFR §114.10. BCRA's so-called Wellstone Amendment applied §441b's expenditure ban to all nonprofit corporations. See 2 U. S. C. §441b(c)(6); *McConnell*, 540 U. S., at 209. *McConnell* then interpreted the Wellstone Amendment to retain the *MCFL* exemption to §441b's expenditure prohibition. 540 U. S., at 211. Citizens United does not qualify for the *MCFL* exemption, however, since some funds used to make the movie were donations from for-profit corporations.

The Government suggests we could find BCRA's Wellstone Amendment unconstitutional, sever it from the statute, and hold that Citizens United's speech is exempt from §441b's ban under BCRA's Snowe-Jeffords Amendment, §441b(c)(2). See Tr. of Oral Arg. 37–38 (Sept. 9, 2009). The Snowe-Jeffords Amendment operates as a backup provision that only takes effect if the Wellstone

Amendment is invalidated. See *McConnell, supra,* at 339 (KENNEDY, J., concurring in judgment in part and dissenting in part). The Snowe-Jeffords Amendment would exempt from §441b's expenditure ban the political speech of certain nonprofit corporations if the speech were funded "exclusively" by individual donors and the funds were maintained in a segregated account. §441b(c)(2). Citizens United would not qualify for the Snowe-Jeffords exemption, under its terms as written, because *Hillary* was funded in part with donations from for-profit corporations.

Consequently, to hold for Citizens United on this argument, the Court would be required to revise the text of *MCFL,* sever BCRA's Wellstone Amendment, §441b(c)(6), and ignore the plain text of BCRA's Snowe-Jeffords Amendment, §441b(c)(2). If the Court decided to create a *de minimis* exception to *MCFL* or the Snowe-Jeffords Amendment, the result would be to allow for-profit corporate general treasury funds to be spent for independent expenditures that support candidates. There is no principled basis for doing this without rewriting *Austin's* holding that the Government can restrict corporate independent expenditures for political speech.

Though it is true that the Court should construe statutes as necessary to avoid constitutional questions, the series of steps suggested would be difficult to take in view of the language of the statute. In addition to those difficulties the Government's suggestion is troubling for still another reason. The Government does not say that it agrees with the interpretation it wants us to consider. See Supp. Brief for Appellee 3, n. 1 ("Some courts" have implied a *de minimis* exception, and "appellant would appear to be covered by these decisions"). Presumably it would find textual difficulties in this approach too. The Government, like any party, can make arguments in the alternative; but it ought to say if there is merit to an alternative proposal instead of merely suggesting it. This is especially true in the context of the First Amendment. As the Government stated, this case "would require a remand" to apply a *de minimis* standard. Tr. of Oral Arg. 39 (Sept. 9, 2009). Applying this standard would thus require case-by-case determinations. But archetypical political speech would be chilled in the meantime. "'First Amendment freedoms need breathing space to survive.'" *WRTL, supra,* at 468–469 (opinion of ROBERTS, C. J.) (quoting *NAACP* v. *Button,* 371 U. S. 415, 433 (1963)). We decline to adopt an interpretation that requires intricate case-by-case determinations to verify whether political speech is banned, especially if we are convinced that, in the end, this corporation has a constitutional right to speak on this subject.

E

As the foregoing analysis confirms, the Court cannot resolve this case on a narrower ground without chilling political speech, speech that is central to the meaning and purpose of the First Amendment. See *Morse* v. *Frederick,* 551 U. S. 393, 403 (2007). It is not judicial restraint to accept an unsound, narrow argument just so the Court can avoid another argument with broader implications. Indeed, a court would be remiss in performing its duties were it to accept an unsound principle merely to avoid the necessity of making a broader ruling. Here, the lack of a valid basis for an alternative ruling requires full consideration of the continuing effect of the speech suppression upheld in *Austin.*

Citizens United stipulated to dismissing count 5 of its complaint, which raised a facial challenge to §441b, even though count 3 raised an as-applied challenge. See App. 23a (count 3: "As applied to *Hillary,* [§441b] is unconstitutional under the First Amendment guarantees of free expression and association"). The Government argues that Citizens United waived its challenge to *Austin* by dismissing count 5. We disagree.

First, even if a party could somehow waive a facial challenge while preserving an as-applied challenge, that would not prevent the Court from reconsidering *Austin* or addressing the facial validity of §441b in this case. "Our practice 'permit[s] review of an issue not pressed [below] so long as it has been passed upon . . . .'" *Lebron*, 513 U. S., at 379 (quoting *United States* v. *Williams*, 504 U. S. 36, 41 (1992); first alteration in original). And here, the District Court addressed Citizens United's facial challenge. See 530 F. Supp. 2d, at 278 ("Citizens wants us to enjoin the operation of BCRA §203 as a facially unconstitutional burden on the First Amendment right to freedom of speech"). In rejecting the claim, it noted that it "would have to overrule *McConnell*" for Citizens United to prevail on its facial challenge and that "[o]nly the Supreme Court may overrule its decisions." *Ibid.* (citing *Rodriguez de Quijas* v. *Shearson/American Express, Inc.*, 490 U. S. 477, 484 (1989)). The District Court did not provide much analysis regarding the facial challenge because it could not ignore the controlling Supreme Court decisions in *Austin* or *McConnell*. Even so, the District Court did "'pas[s] upon'" the issue. *Lebron, supra*, at 379. Furthermore, the District Court's later opinion, which granted the FEC summary judgment, was "[b]ased on the reasoning of [its] prior opinion," which included the discussion of the facial challenge. App. 261a (citing 530 F. Supp. 2d 274). After the District Court addressed the facial validity of the statute, Citizens United raised its challenge to *Austin* in this Court. See Brief for Appellant 30 ("*Austin* was wrongly decided and should be overruled"); *id.*, at 30–32. In these circumstances, it is necessary to consider Citizens United's challenge to *Austin* and the facial validity of §441b's expenditure ban.

Second, throughout the litigation, Citizens United has asserted a claim that the FEC has violated its First Amendment right to free speech. All concede that this claim is properly before us. And "'[o]nce a federal claim is properly presented, a party can make any argument in support of that claim; parties are not limited to the precise arguments they made below.'" *Lebron, supra,* at 379 (quoting *Yee* v. *Escondido,* 503 U. S. 519, 534 (1992); alteration in original). Citizens United's argument that *Austin* should be overruled is "not a new claim." *Lebron,* 513 U. S., at 379. Rather, it is—at most—"a new argument to support what has been [a] consistent claim: that [the FEC] did not accord [Citizens United] the rights it was obliged to provide by the First Amendment." *Ibid.*

Third, the distinction between facial and as-applied challenges is not so well defined that it has some automatic effect or that it must always control the pleadings and disposition in every case involving a constitutional challenge. The distinction is both instructive and necessary, for it goes to the breadth of the remedy employed by the Court, not what must be pleaded in a complaint. See *United States* v. *Treasury Employees,* 513 U. S. 454, 477–478 (1995) (contrasting "a facial challenge" with "a narrower remedy"). The parties cannot enter into a stipulation that prevents the Court from considering certain remedies if those remedies are necessary to resolve a claim that has been preserved. Citizens United has preserved its First Amendment challenge to §441b as applied to the facts of its case; and given all the circumstances, we cannot easily address that issue without assuming a premise—the permissibility of restricting corporate political speech—that is itself in doubt. See Fallon, As-Applied and Facial Challenges and Third-Party Standing, 113 Harv. L. Rev. 1321, 1339 (2000) ("[O]nce a case is brought, no general categorical line bars a court from making broader pronouncements of invalidity in properly 'as-applied' cases"); *id.,* at 1327–1328. As our request for supplemental briefing implied, Citizens United's claim implicates the validity of *Austin,* which in turn implicates the facial validity of §441b.

When the statute now at issue came before the Court in *McConnell*, both the majority and the dissenting opinions considered the question of its facial validity. The holding and validity of *Austin* were essential to the reasoning of the *McConnell* majority opinion, which upheld BCRA's extension of §441b. See 540 U. S., at 205 (quoting *Austin*, 494 U. S., at 660). *McConnell* permitted federal felony punishment for speech by all corporations, including nonprofit ones, that speak on prohibited subjects shortly before federal elections. See 540 U. S., at 203–209. Four Members of the *McConnell* Court would have overruled *Austin*, including Chief Justice Rehnquist, who had joined the Court's opinion in *Austin* but reconsidered that conclusion. See 540 U. S., at 256–262 (SCALIA, J., concurring in part, concurring in judgment in part, and dissenting in part); *id.*, at 273–275 (THOMAS, J., concurring in part, concurring in result in part, concurring in judgment in part, and dissenting in part); *id.*, at 322–338 (opinion of KENNEDY, J., joined by Rehnquist, C. J., and SCALIA, J.). That inquiry into the facial validity of the statute was facilitated by the extensive record, which was "over 100,000 pages" long, made in the three-judge District Court. *McConnell* v. *Federal Election Comm'n*, 251 F. Supp. 2d 176, 209 (DC 2003) *(per curiam) (McConnell I)*. It is not the case, then, that the Court today is premature in interpreting §441b "'on the basis of [a] factually barebones recor[d].'" *Washington State Grange* v. *Washington State Republican Party*, 552 U. S. 442, 450 (2008) (quoting *Sabri* v. *United States*, 541 U. S. 600, 609 (2004)).

The *McConnell* majority considered whether the statute was facially invalid. An as-applied challenge was brought in *Wisconsin Right to Life, Inc.* v. *Federal Election Comm'n*, 546 U. S. 410, 411–412 (2006) *(per curiam)*, and the Court confirmed that the challenge could be maintained. Then, in *WRTL*, the controlling opinion of the

Court not only entertained an as-applied challenge but also sustained it. Three Justices noted that they would continue to maintain the position that the record in *McConnell* demonstrated the invalidity of the Act on its face. 551 U. S., at 485–504 (opinion of SCALIA, J.). The controlling opinion in *WRTL*, which refrained from holding the statute invalid except as applied to the facts then before the Court, was a careful attempt to accept the essential elements of the Court's opinion in *McConnell*, while vindicating the First Amendment arguments made by the *WRTL* parties. 551 U. S., at 482 (opinion of ROBERTS, C. J.).

As noted above, Citizens United's narrower arguments are not sustainable under a fair reading of the statute. In the exercise of its judicial responsibility, it is necessary then for the Court to consider the facial validity of §441b. Any other course of decision would prolong the substantial, nation-wide chilling effect caused by §441b's prohibitions on corporate expenditures. Consideration of the facial validity of §441b is further supported by the following reasons.

First is the uncertainty caused by the litigating position of the Government. As discussed above, see Part II–D, *supra*, the Government suggests, as an alternative argument, that an as-applied challenge might have merit. This argument proceeds on the premise that the nonprofit corporation involved here may have received only *de minimis* donations from for-profit corporations and that some nonprofit corporations may be exempted from the operation of the statute. The Government also suggests that an as-applied challenge to §441b's ban on books may be successful, although it would defend §441b's ban as applied to almost every other form of media including pamphlets. See Tr. of Oral Arg. 65–66 (Sept. 9, 2009). The Government thus, by its own position, contributes to the uncertainty that §441b causes. When the Government holds out the possibility of ruling for Citizens United on a narrow ground yet refrains from adopting that position, the added uncertainty demonstrates the necessity to address the question of statutory validity.

Second, substantial time would be required to bring clarity to the application of the statutory provision on these points in order to avoid any chilling effect caused by some improper interpretation. See Part II–C, *supra*. It is well known that the public begins to concentrate on elections only in the weeks immediately before they are held. There are short timeframes in which speech can have influence. The need or relevance of the speech will often first be apparent at this stage in the campaign. The decision to speak is made in the heat of political campaigns, when speakers react to messages conveyed by others. A speaker's ability to engage in political speech that could have a chance of persuading voters is stifled if the speaker must first commence a protracted lawsuit. By the time the lawsuit concludes, the election will be over and the litigants in most cases will have neither the incentive nor, perhaps, the resources to carry on, even if they could establish that the case is not moot because the issue is "capable of repetition, yet evading review." *WRTL, supra*, at 462 (opinion of ROBERTS, C. J.) (citing *Los Angeles* v. *Lyons*, 461 U. S. 95, 109 (1983); *Southern Pacific Terminal Co.* v. *ICC*, 219 U. S. 498, 515 (1911)). Here, Citizens United decided to litigate its case to the end. Today, Citizens United finally learns, two years after the fact, whether it could have spoken during the 2008 Presidential primary—long after the opportunity to persuade primary voters has passed.

Third is the primary importance of speech itself to the integrity of the election process. As additional rules are created for regulating political speech, any speech arguably within their reach is chilled. See Part II–A, *supra*. Campaign finance regulations now impose "unique and complex rules" on "71 distinct entities." Brief for Seven Former Chairmen of FEC et al. as *Amici Curiae* 11–12. These entities are subject to separate rules for 33 different types of political speech. *Id.,* at 14–15, n. 10. The FEC has adopted 568 pages of regulations, 1,278 pages of explanations and justifications for those regulations, and 1,771 advisory opinions since 1975. See *id.,* at 6, n. 7. In fact, after this Court in *WRTL* adopted an objective "appeal to vote" test for determining whether a communication was the functional equivalent of express advocacy, 551 U. S., at 470 (opinion of ROBERTS, C. J.), the FEC adopted a two-part, 11-factor balancing test to implement *WRTL*'s ruling. See 11 CFR §114.15; Brief for Wyoming Liberty Group et al. as *Amici Curiae* 17–27 (filed Jan. 15, 2009).

This regulatory scheme may not be a prior restraint on speech in the strict sense of that term, for prospective speakers are not compelled by law to seek an advisory opinion from the FEC before the speech takes place. Cf. *Near* v. *Minnesota ex rel. Olson,* 283 U. S. 697, 712–713 (1931). As a practical matter, however, given the complexity of the regulations and the deference courts show to administrative determinations, a speaker who wants to avoid threats of criminal liability and the heavy costs of defending against FEC enforcement must ask a governmental agency for prior permission to speak. See 2 U. S. C. §437f; 11 CFR §112.1. These onerous restrictions thus function as the equivalent of prior restraint by giving the FEC power analogous to licensing laws implemented in 16th- and 17th-century England, laws and governmental practices of the sort that the First Amendment was drawn to prohibit. See *Thomas* v. *Chicago Park Dist.,* 534 U. S. 316, 320 (2002); *Lovell* v. *City of Griffin,* 303 U. S. 444, 451–452 (1938); *Near, supra,* at 713–714. Because the FEC's "business is to censor, there inheres the danger that [it] may well be less responsive than a court—part of an independent branch of government—to the constitutionally protected interests in free expression." *Freedman* v. *Maryland*, 380 U. S. 51, 57–58 (1965). When the FEC issues advisory opinions that prohibit speech, "[m]any persons, rather than undertake the considerable burden (and sometimes risk) of vindicating their rights through case-by-case litigation, will choose simply to abstain from protected speech—harming not only themselves but society as a whole, which is deprived of an uninhibited marketplace of ideas." *Virginia* v. *Hicks*, 539 U. S. 113, 119 (2003) (citation omitted). Consequently, "the censor's determination may in practice be final." *Freedman, supra,* at 58.

This is precisely what *WRTL* sought to avoid. *WRTL* said that First Amendment standards "must eschew 'the open-ended rough-and-tumble of factors,' which 'invit[es] complex argument in a trial court and a virtually inevitable appeal.'" 551 U. S., at 469 (opinion of ROBERTS, C. J.) (quoting *Jerome B. Grubart, Inc.* v. *Great Lakes Dredge & Dock Co.*, 513 U. S. 527, 547 (1995); alteration in original). Yet, the FEC has created a regime that allows it to select what political speech is safe for public consumption by applying ambiguous tests. If parties want to avoid litigation and the possibility of civil and criminal penalties, they must either refrain from speaking or ask the FEC to issue an advisory opinion approving of the political speech in question. Government officials pore over each word of a text to see if, in their judgment, it accords with the 11-factor test they have promulgated. This is an unprecedented governmental intervention into the realm of speech.

The ongoing chill upon speech that is beyond all doubt protected makes it necessary in this case to invoke the earlier precedents that a statute which chills speech can and must be invalidated where its facial invalidity has been demonstrated. See *WRTL, supra,* at 482–483 (ALITO,

J., concurring); *Thornhill* v. *Alabama,* 310 U. S. 88, 97–98 (1940). For these reasons we find it necessary to reconsider *Austin.*

III

The First Amendment provides that "Congress shall make no law . . . abridging the freedom of speech." Laws enacted to control or suppress speech may operate at different points in the speech process. The following are just a few examples of restrictions that have been attempted at different stages of the speech process—all laws found to be invalid: restrictions requiring a permit at the outset, *Watchtower Bible & Tract Soc. of N. Y., Inc.* v. *Village of Stratton,* 536 U. S. 150, 153 (2002); imposing a burden by impounding proceeds on receipts or royalties, *Simon & Schuster, Inc.* v. *Members of N. Y. State Crime Victims Bd.,* 502 U. S. 105, 108, 123 (1991); seeking to exact a cost after the speech occurs, *New York Times Co.* v. *Sullivan,* 376 U. S., at 267; and subjecting the speaker to criminal penalties, *Brandenburg* v. *Ohio,* 395 U. S. 444, 445 (1969) *(per curiam).*

The law before us is an outright ban, backed by criminal sanctions. Section 441b makes it a felony for all corporations—including nonprofit advocacy corporations—either to expressly advocate the election or defeat of candidates or to broadcast electioneering communications within 30 days of a primary election and 60 days of a general election. Thus, the following acts would all be felonies under §441b: The Sierra Club runs an ad, within the crucial phase of 60 days before the general election, that exhorts the public to disapprove of a Congressman who favors logging in national forests; the National Rifle Association publishes a book urging the public to vote for the challenger because the incumbent U. S. Senator supports a handgun ban; and the American Civil Liberties Union creates a Web site telling the public to vote for a Presidential candidate in light of that candidate's defense of free speech. These prohibitions are classic examples of censorship.

Section 441b is a ban on corporate speech notwithstanding the fact that a PAC created by a corporation can still speak. See *McConnell*, 540 U. S., at 330–333 (opinion of KENNEDY, J.). A PAC is a separate association from the corporation. So the PAC exemption from §441b's expenditure ban, §441b(b)(2), does not allow corporations to speak. Even if a PAC could somehow allow a corporation to speak—and it does not—the option to form PACs does not alleviate the First Amendment problems with §441b. PACs are burdensome alternatives; they are expensive to administer and subject to extensive regulations. For example, every PAC must appoint a treasurer, forward donations to the treasurer promptly, keep detailed records of the identities of the persons making donations, preserve receipts for three years, and file an organization statement and report changes to this information within 10 days. See *id.*, at 330–332 (quoting *MCFL*, 479 U. S., at 253–254).

And that is just the beginning. PACs must file detailed monthly reports with the FEC, which are due at different times depending on the type of election that is about to occur:

> "'These reports must contain information regarding the amount of cash on hand; the total amount of receipts, detailed by 10 different categories; the identification of each political committee and candidate's authorized or affiliated committee making contributions, and any persons making loans, providing rebates, refunds, dividends, or interest or any other offset to operating expenditures in an aggregate amount over $200; the total amount of all disbursements, detailed by 12 different categories; the names of all authorized

or affiliated committees to whom expenditures aggregating over $200 have been made; persons to whom loan repayments or refunds have been made; the total sum of all contributions, operating expenses, outstanding debts and obligations, and the settlement terms of the retirement of any debt or obligation.'" 540 U. S., at 331–332 (quoting *MCFL, supra,* at 253–254).

PACs have to comply with these regulations just to speak. This might explain why fewer than 2,000 of the millions of corporations in this country have PACs. See Brief for Seven Former Chairmen of FEC et al. as *Amici Curiae* 11 (citing FEC, Summary of PAC Activity 1990–2006, online at http://www.fec.gov/press/press2007/20071009pac/sumhistory.pdf); IRS, Statistics of Income: 2006, Corporation Income Tax Returns 2 (2009) (hereinafter Statistics of Income) (5.8 million for-profit corporations filed 2006 tax returns). PACs, furthermore, must exist before they can speak. Given the onerous restrictions, a corporation may not be able to establish a PAC in time to make its views known regarding candidates and issues in a current campaign.

Section 441b's prohibition on corporate independent expenditures is thus a ban on speech. As a "restriction on the amount of money a person or group can spend on political communication during a campaign," that statute "necessarily reduces the quantity of expression by restricting the number of issues discussed, the depth of their exploration, and the size of the audience reached." *Buckley* v. *Valeo,* 424 U. S. 1, 19 (1976) *(per curiam).* Were the Court to uphold these restrictions, the Government could repress speech by silencing certain voices at any of the various points in the speech process. See *McConnell, supra,* at 251 (opinion of SCALIA, J.) (Government could repress speech by "attacking all levels of the production and dissemination of ideas," for "effective public communication requires the speaker to make use of the services of others"). If §441b applied to individuals, no one would believe that it is merely a time, place, or manner restriction on speech. Its purpose and effect are to silence entities whose voices the Government deems to be suspect.

Speech is an essential mechanism of democracy, for it is the means to hold officials accountable to the people. See *Buckley, supra,* at 14–15 ("In a republic where the people are sovereign, the ability of the citizenry to make informed choices among candidates for office is essential"). The right of citizens to inquire, to hear, to speak, and to use information to reach consensus is a precondition to enlightened self-government and a necessary means to protect it. The First Amendment "'has its fullest and most urgent application' to speech uttered during a campaign for political office." *Eu* v. *San Francisco County Democratic Central Comm.,* 489 U. S. 214, 223 (1989) (quoting *Monitor Patriot Co.* v. *Roy,* 401 U. S. 265, 272 (1971)); see *Buckley, supra,* at 14 ("Discussion of public issues and debate on the qualifications of candidates are integral to the operation of the system of government established by our Constitution").

For these reasons, political speech must prevail against laws that would suppress it, whether by design or inadvertence. Laws that burden political speech are "subject to strict scrutiny," which requires the Government to prove that the restriction "furthers a compelling interest and is narrowly tailored to achieve that interest." *WRTL,* 551 U. S., at 464 (opinion of ROBERTS, C. J.). While it might be maintained that political speech simply cannot be banned or restricted as a categorical matter, see *Simon & Schuster,* 502 U. S., at 124 (KENNEDY, J., concurring in judgment), the quoted language from *WRTL* provides a sufficient framework for protecting the relevant First Amendment interests in this case. We shall employ it here.

Premised on mistrust of governmental power, the First Amendment stands against attempts to disfavor certain subjects or viewpoints. See, *e.g., United States* v. *Playboy Entertainment Group, Inc.,* 529 U. S. 803, 813 (2000) (striking down content-based restriction). Prohibited, too, are restrictions distinguishing among different speakers, allowing speech by some but not others. See *First Nat. Bank of Boston* v. *Bellotti,* 435 U. S. 765, 784 (1978). As instruments to censor, these categories are interrelated: Speech restrictions based on the identity of the speaker are all too often simply a means to control content.

Quite apart from the purpose or effect of regulating content, moreover, the Government may commit a constitutional wrong when by law it identifies certain preferred speakers. By taking the right to speak from some and giving it to others, the Government deprives the disadvantaged person or class of the right to use speech to strive to establish worth, standing, and respect for the speaker's voice. The Government may not by these means deprive the public of the right and privilege to determine for itself what speech and speakers are worthy of consideration. The First Amendment protects speech and speaker, and the ideas that flow from each.

The Court has upheld a narrow class of speech restrictions that operate to the disadvantage of certain persons, but these rulings were based on an interest in allowing governmental entities to perform their functions. See, *e.g., Bethel School Dist. No. 403* v. *Fraser,* 478 U. S. 675, 683 (1986) (protecting the "function of public school education"); *Jones* v. *North Carolina Prisoners' Labor Union, Inc.,* 433 U. S. 119, 129 (1977) (furthering "the legitimate penological objectives of the corrections system" (internal quotation marks omitted)); *Parker* v. *Levy,* 417 U. S. 733, 759 (1974) (ensuring "the capacity of the Government to discharge its [military] responsibilities" (internal quotation marks omitted)); *Civil Service Comm'n* v. *Letter Carriers*, 413 U. S. 548, 557 (1973) ("[F]ederal service should depend upon meritorious performance rather than political service"). The corporate independent expenditures at issue in this case, however, would not interfere with governmental functions, so these cases are inapposite. These precedents stand only for the proposition that there are certain governmental functions that cannot operate without some restrictions on particular kinds of speech. By contrast, it is inherent in the nature of the political process that voters must be free to obtain information from diverse sources in order to determine how to cast their votes. At least before *Austin*, the Court had not allowed the exclusion of a class of speakers from the general public dialogue.

We find no basis for the proposition that, in the context of political speech, the Government may impose restrictions on certain disfavored speakers. Both history and logic lead us to this conclusion.

A

1

The Court has recognized that First Amendment protection extends to corporations. *Bellotti, supra,* at 778, n. 14 (citing *Linmark Associates, Inc.* v. *Willingboro*, 431 U. S. 85 (1977); *Time, Inc.* v. *Firestone*, 424 U. S. 448 (1976); *Doran* v. *Salem Inn, Inc.*, 422 U. S. 922 (1975); *Southeastern Promotions, Ltd.* v. *Conrad*, 420 U. S. 546 (1975); *Cox Broadcasting Corp.* v. *Cohn*, 420 U. S. 469 (1975); *Miami Herald Publishing Co.* v. *Tornillo*, 418 U. S. 241 (1974); *New York Times Co.* v. *United States*, 403 U. S. 713 (1971) *(per curiam); Time, Inc.* v. *Hill*, 385 U. S. 374 (1967); *New York Times Co.* v. *Sullivan*, 376 U. S. 254; *Kingsley Int'l Pictures Corp.* v. *Regents of Univ. of N. Y.*, 360 U. S. 684 (1959); *Joseph Burstyn, Inc.* v. *Wilson*, 343 U. S. 495 (1952)); see, *e.g., Turner Broadcasting System, Inc.* v. *FCC*,

520 U. S. 180 (1997); *Denver Area Ed. Telecommunications Consortium, Inc.* v. *FCC*, 518 U. S. 727 (1996); *Turner*, 512 U. S. 622; *Simon & Schuster*, 502 U. S. 105; *Sable Communications of Cal., Inc.* v. *FCC*, 492 U. S. 115 (1989); *Florida Star* v. *B. J. F.*, 491 U. S. 524 (1989); *Philadelphia Newspapers, Inc.* v. *Hepps*, 475 U. S. 767 (1986); *Landmark Communications, Inc.* v. *Virginia*, 435 U. S. 829 (1978); *Young* v. *American Mini Theatres, Inc.*, 427 U. S. 50 (1976); *Gertz* v. *Robert Welch, Inc.*, 418 U. S. 323 (1974); *Greenbelt Cooperative Publishing Assn., Inc.* v. *Bresler*, 398 U. S. 6 (1970).

This protection has been extended by explicit holdings to the context of political speech. See, *e.g., Button*, 371 U. S., at 428–429; *Grosjean* v. *American Press Co.*, 297 U. S. 233, 244 (1936). Under the rationale of these precedents, political speech does not lose First Amendment protection "simply because its source is a corporation." *Bellotti, supra,* at 784; see *Pacific Gas & Elec. Co.* v. *Public Util. Comm'n of Cal.*, 475 U. S. 1, 8 (1986) (plurality opinion) ("The identity of the speaker is not decisive in determining whether speech is protected. Corporations and other associations, like individuals, contribute to the 'discussion, debate, and the dissemination of information and ideas' that the First Amendment seeks to foster" (quoting *Bellotti*, 435 U. S., at 783)). The Court has thus rejected the argument that political speech of corporations or other associations should be treated differently under the First Amendment simply because such associations are not "natural persons." *Id.,* at 776; see *id.,* at 780, n. 16. Cf. *id.,* at 828 (Rehnquist, J., dissenting).

At least since the latter part of the 19th century, the laws of some States and of the United States imposed a ban on corporate direct contributions to candidates. See B. Smith, Unfree Speech: The Folly of Campaign Finance Reform 23 (2001). Yet not until 1947 did Congress first prohibit independent expenditures by corporations and labor unions in §304 of the Labor Management Relations Act 1947, 61 Stat. 159 (codified at 2 U. S. C. §251 (1946 ed., Supp. I)). In passing this Act Congress overrode the veto of President Truman, who warned that the expenditure ban was a "dangerous intrusion on free speech." Message from the President of the United States, H. R. Doc. No. 334, 89th Cong., 1st Sess., 9 (1947).

For almost three decades thereafter, the Court did not reach the question whether restrictions on corporate and union expenditures are constitutional. See *WRTL*, 551 U. S., at 502 (opinion of SCALIA, J.). The question was in the background of *United States* v. *CIO*, 335 U. S. 106 (1948). There, a labor union endorsed a congressional candidate in its weekly periodical. The Court stated that "the gravest doubt would arise in our minds as to [the federal expenditure prohibition's] constitutionality" if it were construed to suppress that writing. *Id.*, at 121. The Court engaged in statutory interpretation and found the statute did not cover the publication. *Id.*, at 121–122, and n. 20. Four Justices, however, said they would reach the constitutional question and invalidate the Labor Management Relations Act's expenditure ban. *Id.*, at 155 (Rutledge, J., joined by Black, Douglas, and Murphy, JJ., concurring in result). The concurrence explained that any "'undue influence'" generated by a speaker's "large expenditures" was outweighed "by the loss for democratic processes resulting from the restrictions upon free and full public discussion." *Id.*, at 143.

In *United States* v. *Automobile Workers*, 352 U. S. 567 (1957), the Court again encountered the independent expenditure ban, which had been recodified at 18 U. S. C. §610 (1952 ed.). See 62 Stat. 723–724. After holding only that a union television broadcast that endorsed candidates was covered by the statute, the Court "[r]efus[ed] to anticipate constitutional questions" and remanded for the trial to proceed. 352 U. S., at 591. Three Justices dissented, arguing that the Court should have reached the constitutional question and that the ban on independent expenditures was unconstitutional:

> "Under our Constitution it is We The People who are sovereign. The people have the final say. The legislators are their spokesmen. The people determine through their votes the destiny of the nation. It is therefore important—vitally important—that all channels of communications be open to them during every election, that no point of view be restrained or barred, and that the people have access to the views of every group in the community." *Id.*, at 593 (opinion of Douglas, J., joined by Warren, C. J., and Black, J.).

The dissent concluded that deeming a particular group "too powerful" was not a "justificatio[n] for withholding First Amendment rights from any group—labor or corporate." *Id.*, at 597. The Court did not get another opportunity to consider the constitutional question in that case; for after a remand, a jury found the defendants not guilty. See Hayward, Revisiting the Fable of Reform, 45 Harv. J. Legis. 421, 463 (2008).

Later, in *Pipefitters* v. *United States,* 407 U. S. 385, 400–401 (1972), the Court reversed a conviction for expenditure of union funds for political speech—again without reaching the constitutional question. The Court would not resolve that question for another four years.

2

In *Buckley,* 424 U. S. 1, the Court addressed various challenges to the Federal Election Campaign Act of 1971 (FECA) as amended in 1974. These amendments created 18 U. S. C. §608(e) (1970 ed., Supp. V), see 88 Stat. 1265, an independent expenditure ban separate from §610 that applied to individuals as well as corporations and labor unions, *Buckley,* 424 U. S., at 23, 39, and n. 45.

Before addressing the constitutionality of §608(e)'s independent expenditure ban, *Buckley* first upheld §608(b), FECA's limits on direct contributions to candidates. The *Buckley* Court recognized a "sufficiently important" governmental interest in "the prevention of corruption and the appearance of corruption." *Id.*, at 25; see *id.*, at 26. This followed from the Court's concern that large contributions could be given "to secure a political *quid pro quo*." *Ibid.*

The *Buckley* Court explained that the potential for *quid pro quo* corruption distinguished direct contributions to candidates from independent expenditures. The Court emphasized that "the independent expenditure ceiling . . . fails to serve any substantial governmental interest in stemming the reality or appearance of corruption in the electoral process," *id.*, at 47–48, because "[t]he absence of prearrangement and coordination . . . alleviates the danger that expenditures will be given as a *quid pro quo* for improper commitments from the candidate," *id.*, at 47. *Buckley* invalidated §608(e)'s restrictions on independent expenditures, with only one Justice dissenting. See *Federal Election Comm'n* v. *National Conservative Political Action Comm.*, 470 U. S. 480, 491, n. 3 (1985) *(NCPAC)*.

Buckley did not consider §610's separate ban on corporate and union independent expenditures, the prohibition that had also been in the background in *CIO*, *Automobile Workers*, and *Pipefitters*. Had §610 been challenged in the wake of *Buckley*, however, it could not have been squared with the reasoning and analysis of that precedent. See *WRTL*, *supra*, at 487 (opinion of SCALIA, J.) ("*Buckley* might well have been the last word on limitations on independent expenditures"); *Austin*, 494 U. S., at 683 (SCALIA, J., dissenting). The expenditure ban invalidated in *Buckley*, §608(e), applied to corporations and unions, 424 U. S., at 23, 39, n. 45; and some of the prevailing plaintiffs in *Buckley* were corporations, *id.*, at 8. The

Buckley Court did not invoke the First Amendment's overbreadth doctrine, see *Broadrick* v. *Oklahoma*, 413 U. S. 601, 615 (1973), to suggest that §608(e)'s expenditure ban would have been constitutional if it had applied only to corporations and not to individuals, 424 U. S., at 50. *Buckley* cited with approval the *Automobile Workers* dissent, which argued that §610 was unconstitutional. 424 U. S., at 43 (citing 352 U. S., at 595–596 (opinion of Douglas, J.)).

Notwithstanding this precedent, Congress recodified §610's corporate and union expenditure ban at 2 U. S. C. §441b four months after *Buckley* was decided. See 90 Stat. 490. Section 441b is the independent expenditure restriction challenged here.

Less than two years after *Buckley*, *Bellotti*, 435 U. S. 765, reaffirmed the First Amendment principle that the Government cannot restrict political speech based on the speaker's corporate identity. *Bellotti* could not have been clearer when it struck down a state-law prohibition on corporate independent expenditures related to referenda issues:

> "We thus find no support in the First . . . Amendment, or in the decisions of this Court, for the proposition that speech that otherwise would be within the protection of the First Amendment loses that protection simply because its source is a corporation that cannot prove, to the satisfaction of a court, a material effect on its business or property. . . . [That proposition] amounts to an impermissible legislative prohibition of speech based on the identity of the interests that spokesmen may represent in public debate over controversial issues and a requirement that the speaker have a sufficiently great interest in the subject to justify communication.

"In the realm of protected speech, the legislature is constitutionally disqualified from dictating the subjects about which persons may speak and the speakers who may address a public issue." *Id.*, at 784–785.

It is important to note that the reasoning and holding of *Bellotti* did not rest on the existence of a viewpoint-discriminatory statute. It rested on the principle that the Government lacks the power to ban corporations from speaking.

Bellotti did not address the constitutionality of the State's ban on corporate independent expenditures to support candidates. In our view, however, that restriction would have been unconstitutional under *Bellotti*'s central principle: that the First Amendment does not allow political speech restrictions based on a speaker's corporate identity. See *ibid.*

3

Thus the law stood until *Austin*. *Austin* "uph[eld] a direct restriction on the independent expenditure of funds for political speech for the first time in [this Court's] history." 494 U. S., at 695 (KENNEDY, J., dissenting). There, the Michigan Chamber of Commerce sought to use general treasury funds to run a newspaper ad supporting a specific candidate. Michigan law, however, prohibited corporate independent expenditures that supported or opposed any candidate for state office. A violation of the law was punishable as a felony. The Court sustained the speech prohibition.

To bypass *Buckley* and *Bellotti*, the *Austin* Court identified a new governmental interest in limiting political speech: an antidistortion interest. *Austin* found a compelling governmental interest in preventing "the corrosive and distorting effects of immense aggregations of wealth that are accumulated with the help of the corporate form and that have little or no correlation to the public's support for the corporation's political ideas." 494 U. S., at 660; see *id.*, at 659 (citing *MCFL,* 479 U. S., at 257; *NCPAC,* 470 U. S., at 500–501).

B

The Court is thus confronted with conflicting lines of precedent: a pre-*Austin* line that forbids restrictions on political speech based on the speaker's corporate identity and a post-*Austin* line that permits them. No case before *Austin* had held that Congress could prohibit independent expenditures for political speech based on the speaker's corporate identity. Before *Austin* Congress had enacted legislation for this purpose, and the Government urged the same proposition before this Court. See *MCFL, supra,* at 257 (FEC posited that Congress intended to "curb the political influence of 'those who exercise control over large aggregations of capital'" (quoting *Automobile Workers, supra,* at 585)); *California Medical Assn. v. Federal Election Comm'n,* 453 U. S. 182, 201 (1981) (Congress believed that "differing structures and purposes" of corporations and unions "may require different forms of regulation in order to protect the integrity of the electoral process"). In neither of these cases did the Court adopt the proposition.

In its defense of the corporate-speech restrictions in §441b, the Government notes the antidistortion rationale on which *Austin* and its progeny rest in part, yet it all but abandons reliance upon it. It argues instead that two other compelling interests support *Austin*'s holding that corporate expenditure restrictions are constitutional: an anticorruption interest, see 494 U. S., at 678 (STEVENS, J., concurring), and a shareholder-protection interest, see *id.*, at 674–675 (Brennan, J., concurring). We consider the three points in turn.

1

As for *Austin*'s antidistortion rationale, the Government

does little to defend it. See Tr. of Oral Arg. 45–48 (Sept. 9, 2009). And with good reason, for the rationale cannot support §441b.

If the First Amendment has any force, it prohibits Congress from fining or jailing citizens, or associations of citizens, for simply engaging in political speech. If the antidistortion rationale were to be accepted, however, it would permit Government to ban political speech simply because the speaker is an association that has taken on the corporate form. The Government contends that *Austin* permits it to ban corporate expenditures for almost all forms of communication stemming from a corporation. See Part II–E, *supra;* Tr. of Oral Arg. 66 (Sept. 9, 2009); see also *id.*, at 26–31 (Mar. 24, 2009). If *Austin* were correct, the Government could prohibit a corporation from expressing political views in media beyond those presented here, such as by printing books. The Government responds "that the FEC has never applied this statute to a book," and if it did, "there would be quite [a] good as-applied challenge." Tr. of Oral Arg. 65 (Sept. 9, 2009). This troubling assertion of brooding governmental power cannot be reconciled with the confidence and stability in civic discourse that the First Amendment must secure.

Political speech is "indispensable to decisionmaking in a democracy, and this is no less true because the speech comes from a corporation rather than an individual." *Bellotti*, 435 U. S., at 777 (footnote omitted); see *ibid.* (the worth of speech "does not depend upon the identity of its source, whether corporation, association, union, or individual"); *Buckley*, 424 U. S., at 48–49 ("[T]he concept that government may restrict the speech of some elements of our society in order to enhance the relative voice of others is wholly foreign to the First Amendment"); *Automobile Workers,* 352 U. S., at 597 (Douglas, J., dissenting); *CIO*, 335 U. S., at 154–155 (Rutledge, J., concurring in result). This protection for speech is inconsistent with *Austin's* antidistortion rationale. *Austin* sought to defend the antidistortion rationale as a means to prevent corporations from obtaining "'an unfair advantage in the political marketplace'" by using "'resources amassed in the economic marketplace.'" 494 U. S., at 659 (quoting *MCFL*, *supra*, at 257). But *Buckley* rejected the premise that the Government has an interest "in equalizing the relative ability of individuals and groups to influence the outcome of elections." 424 U. S., at 48; see *Bellotti, supra,* at 791, n. 30. *Buckley* was specific in stating that "the skyrocketing cost of political campaigns" could not sustain the governmental prohibition. 424 U. S., at 26. The First Amendment's protections do not depend on the speaker's "financial ability to engage in public discussion." *Id.*, at 49.

The Court reaffirmed these conclusions when it invalidated the BCRA provision that increased the cap on contributions to one candidate if the opponent made certain expenditures from personal funds. See *Davis* v. *Federal Election Comm'n*, 554 U. S. ___, ___ (2008) (slip op., at 16) ("Leveling electoral opportunities means making and implementing judgments about which strengths should be permitted to contribute to the outcome of an election. The Constitution, however, confers upon voters, not Congress, the power to choose the Members of the House of Representatives, Art. I, §2, and it is a dangerous business for Congress to use the election laws to influence the voters' choices"). The rule that political speech cannot be limited based on a speaker's wealth is a necessary consequence of the premise that the First Amendment generally prohibits the suppression of political speech based on the speaker's identity.

Either as support for its antidistortion rationale or as a further argument, the *Austin* majority undertook to distinguish wealthy individuals from corporations on the ground that "[s]tate law grants corporations special advantages—such as limited liability, perpetual life, and favorable treatment of the accumulation and distribution of assets." 494 U. S., at 658–659. This does not suffice, however, to allow laws prohibiting speech. "It is rudimentary that the State cannot exact as the price of those special advantages the forfeiture of First Amendment rights." *Id.*, at 680 (SCALIA, J., dissenting).

It is irrelevant for purposes of the First Amendment that corporate funds may "have little or no correlation to the public's support for the corporation's political ideas." *Id.*, at 660 (majority opinion). All speakers, including individuals and the media, use money amassed from the economic marketplace to fund their speech. The First Amendment protects the resulting speech, even if it was enabled by economic transactions with persons or entities who disagree with the speaker's ideas. See *id.*, at 707 (KENNEDY, J., dissenting) ("Many persons can trace their funds to corporations, if not in the form of donations, then in the form of dividends, interest, or salary").

Austin's antidistortion rationale would produce the dangerous, and unacceptable, consequence that Congress could ban political speech of media corporations. See *McConnell*, 540 U. S., at 283 (opinion of THOMAS, J.) ("The chilling endpoint of the Court's reasoning is not difficult to foresee: outright regulation of the press"). Cf. *Tornillo*, 418 U. S., at 250 (alleging the existence of "vast accumulations of unreviewable power in the modern media empires"). Media corporations are now exempt from §441b's ban on corporate expenditures. See 2 U. S. C. §§431(9)(B)(i), 434(f)(3)(B)(i). Yet media corporations accumulate wealth with the help of the corporate form, the largest media corporations have "immense aggregations of wealth," and the views expressed by media corporations often "have little or no correlation to the public's support" for those views. *Austin*, 494 U. S., at 660. Thus, under the Government's reasoning, wealthy media corporations could have their voices diminished to put them on par with other media entities. There is no precedent for permitting this under the First Amendment.

The media exemption discloses further difficulties with the law now under consideration. There is no precedent supporting laws that attempt to distinguish between corporations which are deemed to be exempt as media corporations and those which are not. "We have consistently rejected the proposition that the institutional press has any constitutional privilege beyond that of other speakers." *Id.*, at 691 (SCALIA, J., dissenting) (citing *Bellotti,* 435 U. S., at 782); see *Dun & Bradstreet, Inc.* v. *Greenmoss Builders, Inc.,* 472 U. S. 749, 784 (1985) (Brennan, J., joined by Marshall, Blackmun, and STEVENS, JJ., dissenting); *id.,* at 773 (White, J., concurring in judgment). With the advent of the Internet and the decline of print and broadcast media, moreover, the line between the media and others who wish to comment on political and social issues becomes far more blurred.

The law's exception for media corporations is, on its own terms, all but an admission of the invalidity of the antidistortion rationale. And the exemption results in a further, separate reason for finding this law invalid: Again by its own terms, the law exempts some corporations but covers others, even though both have the need or the motive to communicate their views. The exemption applies to media corporations owned or controlled by corporations that have diverse and substantial investments and participate in endeavors other than news. So even assuming the most doubtful proposition that a news organization has a right to speak when others do not, the exemption would allow a conglomerate that owns both a media business and an unrelated business to influence or control the media in order to advance its overall business interest. At the same time, some other corporation, with an identical business interest but no media outlet in its ownership structure, would be forbidden to speak or inform the public about the same issue. This differential treatment cannot be squared with the First Amendment.

There is simply no support for the view that the First Amendment, as originally understood, would permit the suppression of political speech by media corporations. The Framers may not have anticipated modern business and media corporations. See *McIntyre* v. *Ohio Elections Comm'n*, 514 U. S. 334, 360–361 (1995) (THOMAS, J., concurring in judgment). Yet television networks and major newspapers owned by media corporations have become the most important means of mass communication in modern times. The First Amendment was certainly not understood to condone the suppression of political speech in society's most salient media. It was understood as a response to the repression of speech and the press that had existed in England and the heavy taxes on the press that were imposed in the colonies. See *McConnell*, 540 U. S., at 252–253 (opinion of SCALIA, J.); *Grosjean*, 297 U. S., at 245–248; *Near*, 283 U. S., at 713–714. The great debates between the Federalists and the Anti-Federalists over our founding document were published and expressed in the most important means of mass communication of that era—newspapers owned by individuals. See *McIntyre*, 514 U. S., at 341–343; *id.*, at 367 (THOMAS, J., concurring in judgment). At the founding, speech was open, comprehensive, and vital to society's definition of itself; there were no limits on the sources of speech and knowledge. See B. Bailyn, Ideological Origins of the American Revolution 5 (1967) ("Any number of people could join in such proliferating polemics, and rebuttals could come from all sides"); G. Wood, Creation of the American Republic 1776–1787, p. 6 (1969) ("[I]t is not surprising that the intellectual sources of [the Americans'] Revolutionary thought were profuse and various"). The Framers may have been unaware of certain types of speakers or forms of communication, but that does not mean that those speakers and media are entitled to less First Amendment protection than those types of speakers and media that provided the means of communicating political ideas when the Bill of Rights was adopted.

Austin interferes with the "open marketplace" of ideas protected by the First Amendment. *New York State Bd. of Elections* v. *Lopez Torres,* 552 U. S. 196, 208 (2008); see *ibid.* (ideas "may compete" in this marketplace "without government interference"); *McConnell, supra,* at 274 (opinion of THOMAS, J.). It permits the Government to ban the political speech of millions of associations of citizens. See Statistics of Income 2 (5.8 million for-profit corporations filed 2006 tax returns). Most of these are small corporations without large amounts of wealth. See Supp. Brief for Chamber of Commerce of the United States of America as *Amicus Curiae* 1, 3 (96% of the 3 million businesses that belong to the U. S. Chamber of Commerce have fewer than 100 employees); M. Keightley, Congressional Research Service Report for Congress, Business Organizational Choices: Taxation and Responses to Legislative Changes 10 (2009) (more than 75% of corporations whose income is taxed under federal law, see 26 U. S. C. §301, have less than $1 million in receipts per year). This fact belies the Government's argument that the statute is justified on the ground that it prevents the "distorting effects of immense aggregations of wealth." *Austin,* 494 U. S., at 660. It is not even aimed at amassed wealth.

The censorship we now confront is vast in its reach. The Government has "muffle[d] the voices that best represent the most significant segments of the economy." *McConnell, supra,* at 257–258 (opinion of SCALIA, J.). And "the electorate [has been] deprived of information, knowledge and opinion vital to its function." *CIO,* 335 U. S., at 144 (Rutledge, J., concurring in result). By suppressing the speech of manifold corporations, both for-profit and nonprofit, the Government prevents their voices and view-points from reaching the public and advising voters on which persons or entities are hostile to their interests. Factions will necessarily form in our Republic, but the remedy of "destroying the liberty" of some factions is "worse than the disease." The Federalist No. 10, p. 130 (B. Wright ed. 1961) (J. Madison). Factions should be checked by permitting them all to speak, see *ibid.*, and by entrusting the people to judge what is true and what is false.

The purpose and effect of this law is to prevent corporations, including small and nonprofit corporations, from presenting both facts and opinions to the public. This makes *Austin*'s antidistortion rationale all the more an aberration. "[T]he First Amendment protects the right of corporations to petition legislative and administrative bodies." *Bellotti*, 435 U. S., at 792, n. 31 (citing *California Motor Transport Co.* v. *Trucking Unlimited*, 404 U. S. 508, 510–511 (1972); *Eastern Railroad Presidents Conference* v. *Noerr Motor Freight, Inc.*, 365 U. S. 127, 137–138 (1961)). Corporate executives and employees counsel Members of Congress and Presidential administrations on many issues, as a matter of routine and often in private. An *amici* brief filed on behalf of Montana and 25 other States notes that lobbying and corporate communications with elected officials occur on a regular basis. Brief for State of Montana et al. as *Amici Curiae* 19. When that phenomenon is coupled with §441b, the result is that smaller or nonprofit corporations cannot raise a voice to object when other corporations, including those with vast wealth, are cooperating with the Government. That cooperation may sometimes be voluntary, or it may be at the demand of a Government official who uses his or her authority, influence, and power to threaten corporations to support the Government's policies. Those kinds of interactions are often unknown and unseen. The speech that §441b forbids, though, is public, and all can judge its content and purpose. References to massive corporate treasuries should not mask the real operation of this law. Rhetoric ought not obscure reality.

Even if §441b's expenditure ban were constitutional, wealthy corporations could still lobby elected officials, although smaller corporations may not have the resources to do so. And wealthy individuals and unincorporated associations can spend unlimited amounts on independent expenditures. See, *e.g., WRTL*, 551 U. S., at 503–504 (opinion of SCALIA, J.) ("In the 2004 election cycle, a mere 24 individuals contributed an astounding total of $142 million to [26 U. S. C. §527 organizations]"). Yet certain disfavored associations of citizens—those that have taken on the corporate form—are penalized for engaging in the same political speech.

When Government seeks to use its full power, including the criminal law, to command where a person may get his or her information or what distrusted source he or she may not hear, it uses censorship to control thought. This is unlawful. The First Amendment confirms the freedom to think for ourselves.

2

What we have said also shows the invalidity of other arguments made by the Government. For the most part relinquishing the antidistortion rationale, the Government falls back on the argument that corporate political speech can be banned in order to prevent corruption or its appearance. In *Buckley*, the Court found this interest "sufficiently important" to allow limits on contributions but did not extend that reasoning to expenditure limits. 424 U. S., at 25. When *Buckley* examined an expenditure ban, it found "that the governmental interest in preventing corruption and the appearance of corruption [was] inadequate to justify [the ban] on independent expenditures." *Id.,* at 45.

With regard to large direct contributions, *Buckley* reasoned that they could be given "to secure a political *quid pro quo*," *id.*, at 26, and that "the scope of such pernicious practices can never be reliably ascertained," *id.*, at 27. The practices *Buckley* noted would be covered by bribery laws, see, *e.g.*, 18 U. S. C. §201, if a *quid pro quo* arrangement were proved. See *Buckley, supra,* at 27, and n. 28 (citing *Buckley* v. *Valeo,* 519 F. 2d 821, 839–840, and nn. 36–38 (CADC 1975) (en banc) *(per curiam))*. The Court, in consequence, has noted that restrictions on direct contributions are preventative, because few if any contributions to candidates will involve *quid pro quo* arrangements. *MCFL,* 479 U. S., at 260; *NCPAC,* 470 U. S., at 500; *Federal Election Comm'n* v. *National Right to Work Comm.,* 459 U. S. 197, 210 (1982) *(NRWC).* The *Buckley* Court, nevertheless, sustained limits on direct contributions in order to ensure against the reality or appearance of corruption. That case did not extend this rationale to independent expenditures, and the Court does not do so here.

"The absence of prearrangement and coordination of an expenditure with the candidate or his agent not only undermines the value of the expenditure to the candidate, but also alleviates the danger that expenditures will be given as a *quid pro quo* for improper commitments from the candidate." *Buckley,* 424 U. S., at 47; see *ibid.* (independent expenditures have a "substantially diminished potential for abuse"). Limits on independent expenditures, such as §441b, have a chilling effect extending well beyond the Government's interest in preventing *quid pro quo* corruption. The anticorruption interest is not sufficient to displace the speech here in question. Indeed, 26 States do not restrict independent expenditures by for-profit corporations. The Government does not claim that these expenditures have corrupted the political process in those States. See Supp. Brief for Appellee 18, n. 3; Supp. Brief for Chamber of Commerce of the United States of

America as *Amicus Curiae* 8–9, n. 5.

A single footnote in *Bellotti* purported to leave open the possibility that corporate independent expenditures could be shown to cause corruption. 435 U. S., at 788, n. 26. For the reasons explained above, we now conclude that independent expenditures, including those made by corporations, do not give rise to corruption or the appearance of corruption. Dicta in *Bellotti*'s footnote suggested that "a corporation's right to speak on issues of general public interest implies no comparable right in the quite different context of participation in a political campaign for election to public office." *Ibid.* Citing the portion of *Buckley* that invalidated the federal independent expenditure ban, 424 U. S., at 46, and a law review student comment, *Bellotti* surmised that "Congress might well be able to demonstrate the existence of a danger of real or apparent corruption in independent expenditures by corporations to influence candidate elections." 435 U. S., at 788, n. 26. *Buckley*, however, struck down a ban on independent expenditures to support candidates that covered corporations, 424 U. S., at 23, 39, n. 45, and explained that "the distinction between discussion of issues and candidates and advocacy of election or defeat of candidates may often dissolve in practical application," *id.*, at 42. *Bellotti*'s dictum is thus supported only by a law review student comment, which misinterpreted *Buckley*. See Comment, The Regulation of Union Political Activity: Majority and Minority Rights and Remedies, 126 U. Pa. L. Rev. 386, 408 (1977) (suggesting that "corporations and labor unions should be held to different and more stringent standards than an individual or other associations under a regulatory scheme for campaign financing").

Seizing on this aside in *Bellotti*'s footnote, the Court in *NRWC* did say there is a "sufficient" governmental interest in "ensur[ing] that substantial aggregations of wealth amassed" by corporations would not "be used to incur

political debts from legislators who are aided by the contributions." 459 U. S., at 207–208 (citing *Automobile
Workers,* 352 U. S., at 579); see 459 U. S., at 210, and n. 7;
NCPAC, supra, at 500–501 (*NRWC* suggested a governmental interest in restricting "the influence of political
war chests funneled through the corporate form"). *NRWC,*
however, has little relevance here. *NRWC* decided no
more than that a restriction on a corporation's ability to
solicit funds for its segregated PAC, which made direct
contributions to candidates, did not violate the First
Amendment. 459 U. S., at 206. *NRWC* thus involved
contribution limits, see *NCPAC, supra,* at 495–496, which,
unlike limits on independent expenditures, have been an
accepted means to prevent *quid pro quo* corruption, see
McConnell, 540 U. S., at 136–138, and n. 40; *MCFL, supra,* at 259–260. Citizens United has not made direct
contributions to candidates, and it has not suggested that
the Court should reconsider whether contribution limits
should be subjected to rigorous First Amendment scrutiny.

When *Buckley* identified a sufficiently important governmental interest in preventing corruption or the appearance of corruption, that interest was limited to *quid
pro quo* corruption. See *McConnell, supra,* at 296–298
(opinion of KENNEDY, J.) (citing *Buckley, supra,* at 26–28,
30, 46–48); *NCPAC,* 470 U. S., at 497 ("The hallmark of
corruption is the financial *quid pro quo:* dollars for political favors"); *id.,* at 498. The fact that speakers may have
influence over or access to elected officials does not mean
that these officials are corrupt:

> "Favoritism and influence are not . . . avoidable in
> representative politics. It is in the nature of an
> elected representative to favor certain policies, and, by
> necessary corollary, to favor the voters and contribu-
> tors who support those policies. It is well understood
> that a substantial and legitimate reason, if not the

only reason, to cast a vote for, or to make a contribution to, one candidate over another is that the candidate will respond by producing those political outcomes the supporter favors. Democracy is premised on responsiveness." *McConnell*, 540 U. S., at 297 (opinion of KENNEDY, J.).

Reliance on a "generic favoritism or influence theory . . . is at odds with standard First Amendment analyses because it is unbounded and susceptible to no limiting principle." *Id.*, at 296.

The appearance of influence or access, furthermore, will not cause the electorate to lose faith in our democracy. By definition, an independent expenditure is political speech presented to the electorate that is not coordinated with a candidate. See *Buckley*, *supra*, at 46. The fact that a corporation, or any other speaker, is willing to spend money to try to persuade voters presupposes that the people have the ultimate influence over elected officials. This is inconsistent with any suggestion that the electorate will refuse "'to take part in democratic governance'" because of additional political speech made by a corporation or any other speaker. *McConnell*, *supra*, at 144 (quoting *Nixon* v. *Shrink Missouri Government PAC*, 528 U. S. 377, 390 (2000)).

Caperton v. *A. T. Massey Coal Co.*, 556 U. S. ___ (2009), is not to the contrary. *Caperton* held that a judge was required to recuse himself "when a person with a personal stake in a particular case had a significant and disproportionate influence in placing the judge on the case by raising funds or directing the judge's election campaign when the case was pending or imminent." *Id.*, at ___ (slip op., at 14). The remedy of recusal was based on a litigant's due process right to a fair trial before an unbiased judge. See *Withrow* v. *Larkin*, 421 U. S. 35, 46 (1975). *Caperton*'s holding was limited to the rule that the judge must be recused, not that the litigant's political speech could be banned.

The *McConnell* record was "over 100,000 pages" long, *McConnell I*, 251 F. Supp. 2d, at 209, yet it "does not have any direct examples of votes being exchanged for . . . expenditures," *id.*, at 560 (opinion of Kollar-Kotelly, J.). This confirms *Buckley's* reasoning that independent expenditures do not lead to, or create the appearance of, *quid pro quo* corruption. In fact, there is only scant evidence that independent expenditures even ingratiate. See 251 F. Supp. 2d, at 555–557 (opinion of Kollar-Kotelly, J.). Ingratiation and access, in any event, are not corruption. The BCRA record establishes that certain donations to political parties, called "soft money," were made to gain access to elected officials. *McConnell, supra*, at 125, 130–131, 146–152; see *McConnell I*, 251 F. Supp. 2d, at 471–481, 491–506 (opinion of Kollar-Kotelly, J.); *id.*, at 842–843, 858–859 (opinion of Leon, J.). This case, however, is about independent expenditures, not soft money. When Congress finds that a problem exists, we must give that finding due deference; but Congress may not choose an unconstitutional remedy. If elected officials succumb to improper influences from independent expenditures; if they surrender their best judgment; and if they put expediency before principle, then surely there is cause for concern. We must give weight to attempts by Congress to seek to dispel either the appearance or the reality of these influences. The remedies enacted by law, however, must comply with the First Amendment; and, it is our law and our tradition that more speech, not less, is the governing rule. An outright ban on corporate political speech during the critical preelection period is not a permissible remedy. Here Congress has created categorical bans on speech that are asymmetrical to preventing *quid pro quo* corruption.

3

The Government contends further that corporate independent expenditures can be limited because of its interest in protecting dissenting shareholders from being compelled to fund corporate political speech. This asserted interest, like *Austin*'s antidistortion rationale, would allow the Government to ban the political speech even of media corporations. See *supra,* at 35–37. Assume, for example, that a shareholder of a corporation that owns a newspaper disagrees with the political views the newspaper expresses. See *Austin,* 494 U. S., at 687 (SCALIA, J., dissenting). Under the Government's view, that potential disagreement could give the Government the authority to restrict the media corporation's political speech. The First Amendment does not allow that power. There is, furthermore, little evidence of abuse that cannot be corrected by shareholders "through the procedures of corporate democracy." *Bellotti,* 435 U. S., at 794; see *id.,* at 794, n. 34.

Those reasons are sufficient to reject this shareholder-protection interest; and, moreover, the statute is both underinclusive and overinclusive. As to the first, if Congress had been seeking to protect dissenting shareholders, it would not have banned corporate speech in only certain media within 30 or 60 days before an election. A dissenting shareholder's interests would be implicated by speech in any media at any time. As to the second, the statute is overinclusive because it covers all corporations, including nonprofit corporations and for-profit corporations with only single shareholders. As to other corporations, the remedy is not to restrict speech but to consider and explore other regulatory mechanisms. The regulatory mechanism here, based on speech, contravenes the First Amendment.

4

We need not reach the question whether the Govern-

ment has a compelling interest in preventing foreign
individuals or associations from influencing our Nation's
political process. Cf. 2 U. S. C. §441e (contribution and
expenditure ban applied to "foreign national[s]"). Section
441b is not limited to corporations or associations that
were created in foreign countries or funded predominantly
by foreign shareholders. Section 441b therefore would be
overbroad even if we assumed, *arguendo,* that the Government has a compelling interest in limiting foreign
influence over our political process. See *Broadrick,* 413
U. S., at 615.

C

Our precedent is to be respected unless the most convincing of reasons demonstrates that adherence to it puts
us on a course that is sure error. "Beyond workability, the
relevant factors in deciding whether to adhere to the
principle of *stare decisis* include the antiquity of the
precedent, the reliance interests at stake, and of course
whether the decision was well reasoned." *Montejo* v.
Louisiana, 556 U. S. ___, ___ (2009) (slip op., at 13) (overruling *Michigan* v. *Jackson,* 475 U. S. 625 (1986)). We
have also examined whether "experience has pointed up
the precedent's shortcomings." *Pearson* v. *Callahan,* 555
U. S. ___, ___ (2009) (slip op., at 8) (overruling *Saucier* v.
Katz, 533 U. S. 194 (2001)).

These considerations counsel in favor of rejecting *Austin,* which itself contravened this Court's earlier precedents in *Buckley* and *Bellotti.* "This Court has not hesi-
tated to overrule decisions offensive to the First
Amendment." *WRTL,* 551 U. S., at 500 (opinion of SCALIA,
J.). "[S]tare decisis is a principle of policy and not a mechanical formula of adherence to the latest decision."
Helvering v. *Hallock,* 309 U. S. 106, 119 (1940).

For the reasons above, it must be concluded that *Austin*
was not well reasoned. The Government defends *Austin,*

relying almost entirely on "the quid pro quo interest, the corruption interest or the shareholder interest," and not *Austin*'s expressed antidistortion rationale. Tr. of Oral Arg. 48 (Sept. 9, 2009); see *id.,* at 45–46. When neither party defends the reasoning of a precedent, the principle of adhering to that precedent through *stare decisis* is diminished. *Austin* abandoned First Amendment principles, furthermore, by relying on language in some of our precedents that traces back to the *Automobile Workers* Court's flawed historical account of campaign finance laws, see Brief for Campaign Finance Scholars as *Amici Curiae;* Hayward, 45 Harv. J. Legis. 421; R. Mutch, Campaigns, Congress, and Courts 33–35, 153–157 (1988). See *Austin, supra,* at 659 (quoting *MCFL,* 479 U. S., at 257–258; *NCPAC,* 470 U. S., at 500–501); *MCFL, supra,* at 257 (quoting *Automobile Workers,* 352 U. S., at 585); *NCPAC, supra,* at 500 (quoting *NRWC,* 459 U. S., at 210); *id.,* at 208 ("The history of the movement to regulate the political contributions and expenditures of corporations and labor unions is set forth in great detail in *[Automobile Workers], supra,* at 570–584, and we need only summarize the development here").

Austin is undermined by experience since its announcement. Political speech is so ingrained in our culture that speakers find ways to circumvent campaign finance laws. See, *e.g., McConnell,* 540 U. S., at 176–177 ("Given BCRA's tighter restrictions on the raising and spending of soft money, the incentives . . . to exploit [26 U. S. C. §527] organizations will only increase"). Our Nation's speech dynamic is changing, and informative voices should not have to circumvent onerous restrictions to exercise their First Amendment rights. Speakers have become adept at presenting citizens with sound bites, talking points, and scripted messages that dominate the 24-hour news cycle. Corporations, like individuals, do not have monolithic views. On certain topics corporations may possess valuable expertise, leaving them the best equipped to point out errors or fallacies in speech of all sorts, including the speech of candidates and elected officials.

Rapid changes in technology—and the creative dynamic inherent in the concept of free expression—counsel against upholding a law that restricts political speech in certain media or by certain speakers. See Part II–C, *supra.* Today, 30-second television ads may be the most effective way to convey a political message. See *McConnell, supra,* at 261 (opinion of SCALIA, J.). Soon, however, it may be that Internet sources, such as blogs and social networking Web sites, will provide citizens with significant information about political candidates and issues. Yet, §441b would seem to ban a blog post expressly advocating the election or defeat of a candidate if that blog were created with corporate funds. See 2 U. S. C. §441b(a); *MCFL, supra,* at 249. The First Amendment does not permit Congress to make these categorical distinctions based on the corporate identity of the speaker and the content of the political speech.

No serious reliance interests are at stake. As the Court stated in *Payne* v. *Tennessee,* 501 U. S. 808, 828 (1991), reliance interests are important considerations in property and contract cases, where parties may have acted in conformance with existing legal rules in order to conduct transactions. Here, though, parties have been prevented from acting—corporations have been banned from making independent expenditures. Legislatures may have enacted bans on corporate expenditures believing that those bans were constitutional. This is not a compelling interest for *stare decisis.* If it were, legislative acts could prevent us from overruling our own precedents, thereby interfering with our duty "to say what the law is." *Marbury* v. *Madison,* 1 Cranch 137, 177 (1803).

Due consideration leads to this conclusion: *Austin,* 494

U. S. 652, should be and now is overruled. We return to
the principle established in *Buckley* and *Bellotti* that the
Government may not suppress political speech on the
basis of the speaker's corporate identity. No sufficient
governmental interest justifies limits on the political
speech of nonprofit or for-profit corporations.

D

Austin is overruled, so it provides no basis for allowing
the Government to limit corporate independent expenditures. As the Government appears to concede, overruling
Austin "effectively invalidate[s] not only BCRA Section
203, but also 2 U. S. C. 441b's prohibition on the use of
corporate treasury funds for express advocacy." Brief for
Appellee 33, n. 12. Section 441b's restrictions on corporate
independent expenditures are therefore invalid and cannot be applied to *Hillary*.

Given our conclusion we are further required to overrule
the part of *McConnell* that upheld BCRA §203's extension
of §441b's restrictions on corporate independent expenditures. See 540 U. S., at 203–209. The *McConnell* Court
relied on the antidistortion interest recognized in *Austin*
to uphold a greater restriction on speech than the restriction upheld in *Austin*, see 540 U. S., at 205, and we have
found this interest unconvincing and insufficient. This
part of *McConnell* is now overruled.

IV
A

Citizens United next challenges BCRA's disclaimer and
disclosure provisions as applied to *Hillary* and the three
advertisements for the movie. Under BCRA §311, televised electioneering communications funded by anyone
other than a candidate must include a disclaimer that
"'_____ is responsible for the content of this advertising.'" 2 U. S. C. §441d(d)(2). The required statement

must be made in a "clearly spoken manner," and displayed on the screen in a "clearly readable manner" for at least four seconds. *Ibid.* It must state that the communication "is not authorized by any candidate or candidate's committee"; it must also display the name and address (or Web site address) of the person or group that funded the advertisement. §441d(a)(3). Under BCRA §201, any person who spends more than $10,000 on electioneering communications within a calendar year must file a disclosure statement with the FEC. 2 U. S. C. §434(f)(1). That statement must identify the person making the expenditure, the amount of the expenditure, the election to which the communication was directed, and the names of certain contributors. §434(f)(2).

Disclaimer and disclosure requirements may burden the ability to speak, but they "impose no ceiling on campaign-related activities," *Buckley,* 424 U. S., at 64, and "do not prevent anyone from speaking," *McConnell, supra,* at 201 (internal quotation marks and brackets omitted). The Court has subjected these requirements to "exacting scrutiny," which requires a "substantial relation" between the disclosure requirement and a "sufficiently important" governmental interest. *Buckley, supra,* at 64, 66 (internal quotation marks omitted); see *McConnell, supra,* at 231–232.

In *Buckley,* the Court explained that disclosure could be justified based on a governmental interest in "provid[ing] the electorate with information" about the sources of election-related spending. 424 U. S., at 66. The *McConnell* Court applied this interest in rejecting facial challenges to BCRA §§201 and 311. 540 U. S., at 196. There was evidence in the record that independent groups were running election-related advertisements "'while hiding behind dubious and misleading names.'" *Id.,* at 197 (quoting *McConnell I,* 251 F. Supp. 2d, at 237). The Court therefore upheld BCRA §§201 and 311 on the ground that they would help citizens "'make informed choices in the political marketplace.'" 540 U. S., at 197 (quoting *McConnell I, supra,* at 237); see 540 U. S., at 231.

Although both provisions were facially upheld, the Court acknowledged that as-applied challenges would be available if a group could show a "'reasonable probability'" that disclosure of its contributors' names "'will subject them to threats, harassment, or reprisals from either Government officials or private parties.'" *Id.,* at 198 (quoting *Buckley, supra,* at 74).

For the reasons stated below, we find the statute valid as applied to the ads for the movie and to the movie itself.

B

Citizens United sought to broadcast one 30-second and two 10-second ads to promote *Hillary.* Under FEC regulations, a communication that "[p]roposes a commercial transaction" was not subject to 2 U. S. C. §441b's restrictions on corporate or union funding of electioneering communications. 11 CFR §114.15(b)(3)(ii). The regulations, however, do not exempt those communications from the disclaimer and disclosure requirements in BCRA §§201 and 311. See 72 Fed. Reg. 72901 (2007).

Citizens United argues that the disclaimer requirements in §311 are unconstitutional as applied to its ads. It contends that the governmental interest in providing information to the electorate does not justify requiring disclaimers for any commercial advertisements, including the ones at issue here. We disagree. The ads fall within BCRA's definition of an "electioneering communication": They referred to then-Senator Clinton by name shortly before a primary and contained pejorative references to her candidacy. See 530 F. Supp. 2d, at 276, nn. 2–4. The disclaimers required by §311 "provid[e] the electorate with information," *McConnell, supra,* at 196, and "insure that the voters are fully informed" about the person or group who is speaking, *Buckley, supra,* at 76; see also *Bellotti,* 435 U. S., at 792, n. 32 ("Identification of the source of advertising may be required as a means of disclosure, so that the people will be able to evaluate the arguments to which they are being subjected"). At the very least, the disclaimers avoid confusion by making clear that the ads are not funded by a candidate or political party.

Citizens United argues that §311 is underinclusive because it requires disclaimers for broadcast advertisements but not for print or Internet advertising. It asserts that §311 decreases both the quantity and effectiveness of the group's speech by forcing it to devote four seconds of each advertisement to the spoken disclaimer. We rejected these arguments in *McConnell, supra,* at 230–231. And we now adhere to that decision as it pertains to the disclosure provisions.

As a final point, Citizens United claims that, in any event, the disclosure requirements in §201 must be confined to speech that is the functional equivalent of express advocacy. The principal opinion in *WRTL* limited 2 U. S. C. §441b's restrictions on independent expenditures to express advocacy and its functional equivalent. 551 U. S., at 469–476 (opinion of ROBERTS, C. J.). Citizens United seeks to import a similar distinction into BCRA's disclosure requirements. We reject this contention.

The Court has explained that disclosure is a less restrictive alternative to more comprehensive regulations of speech. See, *e.g., MCFL,* 479 U. S., at 262. In *Buckley,* the Court upheld a disclosure requirement for independent expenditures even though it invalidated a provision that imposed a ceiling on those expenditures. 424 U. S., at 75–76. In *McConnell,* three Justices who would have found §441b to be unconstitutional nonetheless voted to uphold BCRA's disclosure and disclaimer requirements. 540 U. S., at 321 (opinion of KENNEDY, J., joined by Rehnquist, C. J., and SCALIA, J.). And the Court has upheld registration and disclosure requirements on lobbyists, even though Congress has no power to ban lobbying itself. *United States* v. *Harriss,* 347 U. S. 612, 625 (1954) (Congress "has merely provided for a modicum of information from those who for hire attempt to influence legislation or who collect or spend funds for that purpose"). For these reasons, we reject Citizens United's contention that the disclosure requirements must be limited to speech that is the functional equivalent of express advocacy.

Citizens United also disputes that an informational interest justifies the application of §201 to its ads, which only attempt to persuade viewers to see the film. Even if it disclosed the funding sources for the ads, Citizens United says, the information would not help viewers make informed choices in the political marketplace. This is similar to the argument rejected above with respect to disclaimers. Even if the ads only pertain to a commercial transaction, the public has an interest in knowing who is speaking about a candidate shortly before an election. Because the informational interest alone is sufficient to justify application of §201 to these ads, it is not necessary to consider the Government's other asserted interests.

Last, Citizens United argues that disclosure requirements can chill donations to an organization by exposing donors to retaliation. Some *amici* point to recent events in which donors to certain causes were blacklisted, threatened, or otherwise targeted for retaliation. See Brief for Institute for Justice as *Amicus Curiae* 13–16; Brief for Alliance Defense Fund as *Amicus Curiae* 16–22. In *McConnell,* the Court recognized that §201 would be unconstitutional as applied to an organization if there were a reasonable probability that the group's members would face threats, harassment, or reprisals if their names were disclosed. 540 U. S., at 198. The examples cited by *amici* are cause for concern. Citizens United, however, has offered no evidence that its members may face similar

threats or reprisals. To the contrary, Citizens United has
been disclosing its donors for years and has identified no
instance of harassment or retaliation.

Shareholder objections raised through the procedures of
corporate democracy, see *Bellotti, supra,* at 794, and n. 34,
can be more effective today because modern technology
makes disclosures rapid and informative. A campaign
finance system that pairs corporate independent expenditures with effective disclosure has not existed before today. It must be noted, furthermore, that many of Congress' findings in passing BCRA were premised on a
system without adequate disclosure. See *McConnell,* 540
U. S., at 128 ("[T]he public may not have been fully informed about the sponsorship of so-called issue ads"); *id.,*
at 196–197 (quoting *McConnell I,* 251 F. Supp. 2d, at 237).
With the advent of the Internet, prompt disclosure of
expenditures can provide shareholders and citizens with
the information needed to hold corporations and elected
officials accountable for their positions and supporters.
Shareholders can determine whether their corporation's
political speech advances the corporation's interest in
making profits, and citizens can see whether elected officials are "'in the pocket' of so-called moneyed interests."
540 U. S., at 259 (opinion of SCALIA, J.); see *MCFL, supra,*
at 261. The First Amendment protects political speech;
and disclosure permits citizens and shareholders to react
to the speech of corporate entities in a proper way. This
transparency enables the electorate to make informed
decisions and give proper weight to different speakers and
messages.

C

For the same reasons we uphold the application of
BCRA §§201 and 311 to the ads, we affirm their application to *Hillary.* We find no constitutional impediment to
the application of BCRA's disclaimer and disclosure re-

quirements to a movie broadcast via video-on-demand. And there has been no showing that, as applied in this case, these requirements would impose a chill on speech or expression.

V

When word concerning the plot of the movie *Mr. Smith Goes to Washington* reached the circles of Government, some officials sought, by persuasion, to discourage its distribution. See Smoodin, "Compulsory" Viewing for Every Citizen: *Mr. Smith* and the Rhetoric of Reception, 35 Cinema Journal 3, 19, and n. 52 (Winter 1996) (citing Mr. Smith Riles Washington, Time, Oct. 30, 1939, p. 49); Nugent, Capra's Capitol Offense, N. Y. Times, Oct. 29, 1939, p. X5. Under *Austin*, though, officials could have done more than discourage its distribution—they could have banned the film. After all, it, like *Hillary,* was speech funded by a corporation that was critical of Members of Congress. *Mr. Smith Goes to Washington* may be fiction and caricature; but fiction and caricature can be a powerful force.

Modern day movies, television comedies, or skits on Youtube.com might portray public officials or public policies in unflattering ways. Yet if a covered transmission during the blackout period creates the background for candidate endorsement or opposition, a felony occurs solely because a corporation, other than an exempt media corporation, has made the "purchase, payment, distribution, loan, advance, deposit, or gift of money or anything of value" in order to engage in political speech. 2 U. S. C. §431(9)(A)(i). Speech would be suppressed in the realm where its necessity is most evident: in the public dialogue preceding a real election. Governments are often hostile to speech, but under our law and our tradition it seems stranger than fiction for our Government to make this political speech a crime. Yet this is the statute's purpose and design.

Some members of the public might consider *Hillary* to be insightful and instructive; some might find it to be neither high art nor a fair discussion on how to set the Nation's course; still others simply might suspend judgment on these points but decide to think more about issues and candidates. Those choices and assessments, however, are not for the Government to make. "The First Amendment underwrites the freedom to experiment and to create in the realm of thought and speech. Citizens must be free to use new forms, and new forums, for the expression of ideas. The civic discourse belongs to the people, and the Government may not prescribe the means used to conduct it." *McConnell, supra,* at 341 (opinion of KENNEDY, J.).

The judgment of the District Court is reversed with respect to the constitutionality of 2 U. S. C. §441b's restrictions on corporate independent expenditures. The judgment is affirmed with respect to BCRA's disclaimer and disclosure requirements. The case is remanded for further proceedings consistent with this opinion.

It is so ordered.

SUPREME COURT OF THE UNITED STATES

No. 08–205

CITIZENS UNITED, APPELLANT *v.* FEDERAL
ELECTION COMMISSION

ON APPEAL FROM THE UNITED STATES DISTRICT COURT FOR
THE DISTRICT OF COLUMBIA

[January 21, 2010]

CHIEF JUSTICE ROBERTS, with whom JUSTICE ALITO
joins, concurring.

The Government urges us in this case to uphold a direct
prohibition on political speech. It asks us to embrace a
theory of the First Amendment that would allow censorship not only of television and radio broadcasts, but of
pamphlets, posters, the Internet, and virtually any other
medium that corporations and unions might find useful in
expressing their views on matters of public concern. Its
theory, if accepted, would empower the Government to
prohibit newspapers from running editorials or opinion
pieces supporting or opposing candidates for office, so long
as the newspapers were owned by corporations—as the
major ones are. First Amendment rights could be confined
to individuals, subverting the vibrant public discourse
that is at the foundation of our democracy.

The Court properly rejects that theory, and I join its
opinion in full. The First Amendment protects more than
just the individual on a soapbox and the lonely pamphle-
teer. I write separately to address the important principles of judicial restraint and *stare decisis* implicated in
this case.

I

Judging the constitutionality of an Act of Congress is

"the gravest and most delicate duty that this Court is called upon to perform." *Blodgett* v. *Holden,* 275 U. S. 142, 147–148 (1927) (Holmes, J., concurring). Because the stakes are so high, our standard practice is to refrain from addressing constitutional questions except when necessary to rule on particular claims before us. See *Ashwander* v. *TVA,* 297 U. S. 288, 346–348 (1936) (Brandeis, J., concurring). This policy underlies both our willingness to construe ambiguous statutes to avoid constitutional problems and our practice "'never to formulate a rule of constitutional law broader than is required by the precise facts to which it is to be applied.'" *United States* v. *Raines,* 362 U. S. 17, 21 (1960) (quoting *Liverpool, New York & Philadelphia S. S. Co.* v. *Commissioners of Emigration,* 113 U. S. 33, 39 (1885)).

The majority and dissent are united in expressing allegiance to these principles. *Ante,* at 12; *post,* at 14 (STEVENS, J., concurring in part and dissenting in part). But I cannot agree with my dissenting colleagues on how these principles apply in this case.

The majority's step-by-step analysis accords with our standard practice of avoiding broad constitutional questions except when necessary to decide the case before us. The majority begins by addressing—and quite properly rejecting—Citizens United's statutory claim that 2 U. S. C. §441b does not actually cover its production and distribution of *Hillary: The Movie* (hereinafter *Hillary*). If there were a valid basis for deciding this statutory claim in Citizens United's favor (and thereby avoiding constitutional adjudication), it would be proper to do so. Indeed, that is precisely the approach the Court took just last Term in *Northwest Austin Municipal Util. Dist. No. One* v. *Holder,* 557 U. S. ___ (2009), when eight Members of the Court agreed to decide the case on statutory grounds instead of reaching the appellant's broader argument that the Voting Rights Act is unconstitutional.

ROBERTS, C. J., concurring

It is only because the majority rejects Citizens United's statutory claim that it proceeds to consider the group's various constitutional arguments, beginning with its narrowest claim (that *Hillary* is not the functional equivalent of express advocacy) and proceeding to its broadest claim (that *Austin* v. *Michigan Chamber of Commerce*, 494 U. S. 652 (1990) should be overruled). This is the same order of operations followed by the controlling opinion in *Federal Election Comm'n* v. *Wisconsin Right to Life, Inc.*, 551 U. S. 449 (2007) (*WRTL*). There the appellant was able to prevail on its narrowest constitutional argument because its broadcast ads did not qualify as the functional equivalent of express advocacy; there was thus no need to go on to address the broader claim that *McConnell* v. *Federal Election Comm'n*, 540 U. S. 93 (2003), should be overruled. *WRTL*, 551 U. S., at 482; *id.*, at 482–483 (ALITO, J., concurring). This case is different—not, as the dissent suggests, because the approach taken in *WRTL* has been deemed a "failure," *post*, at 11, but because, in the absence of any valid narrower ground of decision, there is no way to avoid Citizens United's broader constitutional argument.

The dissent advocates an approach to addressing Citizens United's claims that I find quite perplexing. It presumably agrees with the majority that Citizens United's narrower statutory and constitutional arguments lack merit—otherwise its conclusion that the group should lose this case would make no sense. Despite agreeing that these narrower arguments fail, however, the dissent argues that the majority should nonetheless latch on to one of them in order to avoid reaching the broader constitutional question of whether *Austin* remains good law. It even suggests that the Court's failure to adopt one of these concededly meritless arguments is a sign that the majority is not "serious about judicial restraint." *Post*, at 16.

This approach is based on a false premise: that our

practice of avoiding unnecessary (and unnecessarily broad) constitutional holdings somehow trumps our obligation faithfully to interpret the law. It should go without saying, however, that we cannot embrace a narrow ground of decision simply because it is narrow; it must also be right. Thus while it is true that "[i]f it is not necessary to decide more, it is necessary not to decide more," *post*, at 14 (internal quotation marks omitted), sometimes it *is* necessary to decide more. There is a difference between judicial restraint and judicial abdication. When constitutional questions are "indispensably necessary" to resolving the case at hand, "the court must meet and decide them." *Ex parte Randolph*, 20 F. Cas. 242, 254 (No. 11, 558) (CC Va. 1833) (Marshall, C. J.).

Because it is necessary to reach Citizens United's broader argument that *Austin* should be overruled, the debate over whether to consider this claim on an as-applied or facial basis strikes me as largely beside the point. Citizens United has standing—it is being injured by the Government's enforcement of the Act. Citizens United has a constitutional claim—the Act violates the First Amendment, because it prohibits political speech. The Government has a defense—the Act may be enforced, consistent with the First Amendment, against corporations. Whether the claim or the defense prevails is the question before us.

Given the nature of that claim and defense, it makes no difference of any substance whether this case is resolved by invalidating the statute on its face or only as applied to Citizens United. Even if considered in as-applied terms, a holding in this case that the Act may not be applied to Citizens United—because corporations as well as individuals enjoy the pertinent First Amendment rights— would mean that any other corporation raising the same challenge would also win. Likewise, a conclusion that the Act may be applied to Citizens United—because it is constitutional to prohibit corporate political speech—would similarly govern future cases. Regardless whether we label Citizens United's claim a "facial" or "as-applied" challenge, the consequences of the Court's decision are the same.[1]

II

The text and purpose of the First Amendment point in the same direction: Congress may not prohibit political speech, even if the speaker is a corporation or union. What makes this case difficult is the need to confront our prior decision in *Austin*.

This is the first case in which we have been asked to overrule *Austin*, and thus it is also the first in which we have had reason to consider how much weight to give *stare decisis* in assessing its continued validity. The dissent erroneously declares that the Court "reaffirmed" *Austin*'s holding in subsequent cases—namely, *Federal Election Comm'n* v. *Beaumont*, 539 U. S. 146 (2003); *McConnell*; and *WRTL*. *Post*, at 48–50. Not so. Not a single party in any of those cases asked us to overrule *Austin*, and as the dissent points out, *post*, at 4–6, the Court generally does not consider constitutional arguments that have not properly been raised. *Austin*'s validity was therefore not directly at issue in the cases the dissent cites. The Court's unwillingness to overturn *Austin* in those cases cannot be understood as a *reaffirmation* of that decision.

A

Fidelity to precedent—the policy of *stare decisis*—is vital

---

[1] The dissent suggests that I am "much too quick" to reach this conclusion because I "ignore" Citizens United's narrower arguments. *Post*, at 13, n. 12. But in fact I do not ignore those arguments; on the contrary, I (and my colleagues in the majority) appropriately consider and reject them on their merits, before addressing Citizens United's broader claims. *Supra*, at 2–3; *ante*, at 5–12.

to the proper exercise of the judicial function. "*Stare decisis* is the preferred course because it promotes the evenhanded, predictable, and consistent development of legal principles, fosters reliance on judicial decisions, and contributes to the actual and perceived integrity of the judicial process." *Payne* v. *Tennessee*, 501 U. S. 808, 827 (1991). For these reasons, we have long recognized that departures from precedent are inappropriate in the absence of a "special justification." *Arizona* v. *Rumsey*, 467 U. S. 203, 212 (1984).

At the same time, *stare decisis* is neither an "inexorable command," *Lawrence* v. *Texas*, 539 U. S. 558, 577 (2003), nor "a mechanical formula of adherence to the latest decision," *Helvering* v. *Hallock*, 309 U. S. 106, 119 (1940), especially in constitutional cases, see *United States* v. *Scott*, 437 U. S. 82, 101 (1978). If it were, segregation would be legal, minimum wage laws would be unconstitutional, and the Government could wiretap ordinary criminal suspects without first obtaining warrants. See *Plessy* v. *Ferguson*, 163 U. S. 537 (1896), overruled by *Brown* v. *Board of Education*, 347 U. S. 483 (1954); *Adkins* v. *Children's Hospital of D. C.*, 261 U. S. 525 (1923), overruled by *West Coast Hotel Co.* v. *Parrish*, 300 U. S. 379 (1937); *Olmstead* v. *United States*, 277 U. S. 438 (1928), overruled by *Katz* v. *United States*, 389 U. S. 347 (1967). As the dissent properly notes, none of us has viewed *stare decisis* in such absolute terms. *Post*, at 17; see also, *e.g.*, *Randall* v. *Sorrell*, 548 U. S. 230, 274–281 (2006) (STEVENS, J., dissenting) (urging the Court to overrule its invalidation of limits on independent expenditures on political speech in *Buckley* v. *Valeo*, 424 U. S. 1 (1976) (*per curiam*)).

Stare decisis is instead a "principle of policy." *Helvering, supra*, at 119. When considering whether to reexamine a prior erroneous holding, we must balance the importance of having constitutional questions *decided* against the importance of having them *decided right*. As Justice

Jackson explained, this requires a "sober appraisal of the disadvantages of the innovation as well as those of the questioned case, a weighing of practical effects of one against the other." Jackson, Decisional Law and *Stare Decisis*, 30 A. B. A. J. 334 (1944).

In conducting this balancing, we must keep in mind that *stare decisis* is not an end in itself. It is instead "the means by which we ensure that the law will not merely change erratically, but will develop in a principled and intelligible fashion." *Vasquez* v. *Hillery*, 474 U. S. 254, 265 (1986). Its greatest purpose is to serve a constitutional ideal—the rule of law. It follows that in the unusual circumstance when fidelity to any particular precedent does more to damage this constitutional ideal than to advance it, we must be more willing to depart from that precedent.

Thus, for example, if the precedent under consideration itself departed from the Court's jurisprudence, returning to the " 'intrinsically sounder' doctrine established in prior cases" may "better serv[e] the values of *stare decisis* than would following [the] more recently decided case inconsistent with the decisions that came before it." *Adarand Constructors, Inc.* v. *Peña*, 515 U. S. 200, 231 (1995); see also *Helvering, supra*, at 119; *Randall, supra*, at 274 (STEVENS, J., dissenting). Abrogating the errant precedent, rather than reaffirming or extending it, might better preserve the law's coherence and curtail the precedent's disruptive effects.

Likewise, if adherence to a precedent actually impedes the stable and orderly adjudication of future cases, its *stare decisis* effect is also diminished. This can happen in a number of circumstances, such as when the precedent's validity is so hotly contested that it cannot reliably function as a basis for decision in future cases, when its rationale threatens to upend our settled jurisprudence in related areas of law, and when the precedent's underlying reasoning has become so discredited that the Court cannot keep the precedent alive without jury-rigging new and different justifications to shore up the original mistake. See, *e.g., Pearson* v. *Callahan,* 555 U. S. ___, ___ (2009) (slip op., at 10); *Montejo* v. *Louisiana,* 556 U. S. ___, ___ (2009) (slip op., at 13) (*stare decisis* does not control when adherence to the prior decision requires "fundamentally revising its theoretical basis").

B

These considerations weigh against retaining our decision in *Austin.* First, as the majority explains, that decision was an "aberration" insofar as it departed from the robust protections we had granted political speech in our earlier cases. *Ante,* at 39; see also *Buckley, supra; First Nat. Bank of Boston* v. *Bellotti,* 435 U. S. 765 (1978). *Austin* undermined the careful line that *Buckley* drew to distinguish limits on contributions to candidates from limits on independent expenditures on speech. *Buckley* rejected the asserted government interest in regulating independent expenditures, concluding that "restrict[ing] the speech of some elements of our society in order to enhance the relative voice of others is wholly foreign to the First Amendment." 424 U. S., at 48–49; see also *Bellotti, supra,* at 790–791; *Citizens Against Rent Control/Coalition for Fair Housing* v. *Berkeley,* 454 U. S. 290, 295 (1981). *Austin,* however, allowed the Government to prohibit these same expenditures out of concern for "the corrosive and distorting effects of immense aggregations of wealth" in the marketplace of ideas. 494 U. S., at 660. *Austin*'s reasoning was—and remains—inconsistent with *Buckley*'s explicit repudiation of any government interest in "equalizing the relative ability of individuals and groups to influence the outcome of elections." 424 U. S., at 48–49.

Austin was also inconsistent with *Bellotti*'s clear rejection of the idea that "speech that otherwise would be within the protection of the First Amendment loses that protection simply because its source is a corporation." 435 U. S., at 784. The dissent correctly points out that *Bellotti* involved a referendum rather than a candidate election, and that *Bellotti* itself noted this factual distinction, *id.*, at 788, n. 26; *post*, at 52. But this distinction does not explain why corporations may be subject to prohibitions on speech in candidate elections when individuals may not.

Second, the validity of *Austin*'s rationale—itself adopted over two "spirited dissents," *Payne*, 501 U. S., at 829—has proved to be the consistent subject of dispute among Members of this Court ever since. See, *e.g.*, *WRTL*, 551 U. S., at 483 (SCALIA, J., joined by KENNEDY and THOMAS, JJ., concurring in part and concurring in judgment); *McConnell*, 540 U. S., at 247, 264, 286 (opinions of SCALIA, THOMAS, and KENNEDY, JJ.); *Beaumont*, 539 U. S., at 163, 164 (opinions of KENNEDY and THOMAS, JJ.). The simple fact that one of our decisions remains controversial is, of course, insufficient to justify overruling it. But it does undermine the precedent's ability to contribute to the stable and orderly development of the law. In such circumstances, it is entirely appropriate for the Court—which in this case is squarely asked to reconsider *Austin*'s validity for the first time—to address the matter with a greater willingness to consider new approaches capable of restoring our doctrine to sounder footing.

Third, the *Austin* decision is uniquely destabilizing because it threatens to subvert our Court's decisions even outside the particular context of corporate express advocacy. The First Amendment theory underlying *Austin*'s holding is extraordinarily broad. *Austin*'s logic would authorize government prohibition of political speech by a category of speakers in the name of equality—a point that most scholars acknowledge (and many celebrate), but that the dissent denies. Compare, *e.g.*, Garrett, New Voices in

Politics: Justice Marshall's Jurisprudence on Law and Politics, 52 Howard L. J. 655, 669 (2009) (*Austin* "has been understood by most commentators to be an opinion driven by equality considerations, albeit disguised in the language of 'political corruption' ") with *post*, at 74 (*Austin's* rationale "is manifestly not just an 'equalizing' ideal in disguise").[2]

It should not be surprising, then, that Members of the Court have relied on *Austin's* expansive logic to justify greater incursions on the First Amendment, even outside the original context of corporate advocacy on behalf of candidates running for office. See, *e.g.*, *Davis* v. *Federal Election Comm'n*, 554 U. S. ___, ___ (2008) (slip op., at 7–8) (STEVENS, J., concurring in part and dissenting in part) (relying on *Austin* and other cases to justify restrictions on campaign spending by individual candidates, explaining that "there is no reason that their logic—specifically, their concerns about the corrosive and distorting effects of wealth on our political process—is not equally applicable in the context of individual wealth"); *McConnell, supra*, at 203–209 (extending *Austin* beyond its original context to cover not only the "functional equivalent" of express advocacy by corporations, but also electioneering speech conducted by labor unions). The dissent in this case succumbs to the same temptation, suggesting that *Austin* justifies prohibiting corporate speech because such speech

---

[2] See also, *e.g.*, R. Hasen, The Supreme Court and Election Law: Judging Equality from *Baker* v. *Carr* to *Bush* v. *Gore* 114 (2003) ("*Austin* represents the first and only case [before *McConnell*] in which a majority of the Court accepted, in deed if not in word, the equality rationale as a permissible state interest"); Strauss, Corruption, Equality, and Campaign Finance Reform, 94 Colum. L. Rev. 1369, 1369, and n. 1 (1994) (noting that *Austin's* rationale was based on equalizing political speech); Ashdown, Controlling Campaign Spending and the "New Corruption": Waiting for the Court, 44 Vand. L. Rev. 767, 781 (1991); Eule, Promoting Speaker Diversity: *Austin* and *Metro Broadcasting*, 1990 S. Ct. Rev. 105, 108–111.

might unduly influence "the market for legislation." *Post,*
at 82. The dissent reads *Austin* to permit restrictions on
corporate speech based on nothing more than the fact that
the corporate form may help individuals coordinate and
present their views more effectively. *Post,* at 82. A
speaker's ability to persuade, however, provides no basis
for government regulation of free and open public debate
on what the laws should be.

If taken seriously, *Austin*'s logic would apply most directly to newspapers and other media corporations. They
have a more profound impact on public discourse than
most other speakers. These corporate entities are, for the
time being, not subject to §441b's otherwise generally
applicable prohibitions on corporate political speech. But
this is simply a matter of legislative grace. The fact that
the law currently grants a favored position to media corporations is no reason to overlook the danger inherent in
accepting a theory that would allow government restrictions on their political speech. See generally *McConnell,*
supra, at 283–286 (THOMAS, J., concurring in part, concurring in judgment in part, and dissenting in part).

These readings of *Austin* do no more than carry that
decision's reasoning to its logical endpoint. In doing so,
they highlight the threat *Austin* poses to First Amendment rights generally, even outside its specific factual
context of corporate express advocacy. Because *Austin* is
so difficult to confine to its facts—and because its logic
threatens to undermine our First Amendment jurisprudence and the nature of public discourse more broadly—
the costs of giving it *stare decisis* effect are unusually high.

Finally and most importantly, the Government's own
effort to defend *Austin*—or, more accurately, to defend
something that is not quite *Austin*—underscores its weakness as a precedent of the Court. The Government concedes that *Austin* "is not the most lucid opinion," yet asks
us to reaffirm its holding. Tr. of Oral Arg. 62 (Sept. 9,

2009). But while invoking *stare decisis* to support this position, the Government never once even *mentions* the compelling interest that *Austin* relied upon in the first place: the need to diminish "the corrosive and distorting effects of immense aggregations of wealth that are accumulated with the help of the corporate form and that have little or no correlation to the public's support for the corporation's political ideas." 494 U. S., at 660.

Instead of endorsing *Austin* on its own terms, the Government urges us to reaffirm *Austin*'s specific holding on the basis of two new and potentially expansive interests— the need to prevent actual or apparent *quid pro quo* corruption, and the need to protect corporate shareholders. See Supp. Brief for Appellee 8–10, 12–13. Those interests may or may not support the *result* in *Austin*, but they were plainly not part of the *reasoning* on which *Austin* relied.

To its credit, the Government forthrightly concedes that *Austin* did not embrace either of the new rationales it now urges upon us. See, *e.g.,* Supp. Brief for Appellee 11 ("The Court did not decide in *Austin* . . . whether the compelling interest in preventing actual or apparent corruption provides a constitutionally sufficient justification for prohibiting the use of corporate treasury funds for independent electioneering"); Tr. of Oral Arg. 45 (Sept. 9, 2009) ("*Austin* did not articulate what we believe to be the strongest compelling interest"); *id.,* at 61 ("[The Court:] I take it we have never accepted your shareholder protection interest. This is a new argument. [The Government:] I think that that's fair"); *id.,* at 64 ("[The Court:] In other words, you are asking us to uphold *Austin* on the basis of two arguments, two principles, two compelling interests we have never accepted in [the context of limits on political expenditures]. [The Government:] [I]n this particular context, fair enough").

To be clear: The Court in *Austin* nowhere relied upon the only arguments the Government now raises to support that decision. In fact, the only opinion in *Austin* endorsing the Government's argument based on the threat of *quid pro quo* corruption was JUSTICE STEVENS's concurrence. 494 U. S., at 678. The Court itself did not do so, despite the fact that the concurrence highlighted the argument. Moreover, the Court's only discussion of shareholder protection in *Austin* appeared in a section of the opinion that sought merely to distinguish *Austin*'s facts from those of *Federal Election Comm'n* v. *Massachusetts Citizens for Life, Inc.*, 479 U. S. 238 (1986). *Austin, supra,* at 663. Nowhere did *Austin* suggest that the goal of protecting shareholders is itself a compelling interest authorizing restrictions on First Amendment rights.

To the extent that the Government's case for reaffirming *Austin* depends on radically reconceptualizing its reasoning, that argument is at odds with itself. *Stare decisis* is a doctrine of preservation, not transformation. It counsels deference to past mistakes, but provides no justification for making new ones. There is therefore no basis for the Court to give precedential sway to reasoning that it has never accepted, simply because that reasoning happens to support a conclusion reached on different grounds that have since been abandoned or discredited.

Doing so would undermine the rule-of-law values that justify *stare decisis* in the first place. It would effectively license the Court to invent and adopt new principles of constitutional law solely for the purpose of rationalizing its past errors, without a proper analysis of whether those principles have merit on their own. This approach would allow the Court's past missteps to spawn future mistakes, undercutting the very rule-of-law values that *stare decisis* is designed to protect.

None of this is to say that the Government is barred from making new arguments to support the outcome in *Austin*. On the contrary, it is free to do so. And of course the Court is free to accept them. But the Government's new arguments must stand or fall on their own; they are not entitled to receive the special deference we accord to precedent. They are, as grounds to support *Austin*, literally *un*precedented. Moreover, to the extent the Government relies on new arguments—and declines to defend *Austin* on its own terms—we may reasonably infer that it lacks confidence in that decision's original justification.

Because continued adherence to *Austin* threatens to subvert the "principled and intelligible" development of our First Amendment jurisprudence, *Vasquez*, 474 U. S., at 265, I support the Court's determination to overrule that decision.

*   *   *

We have had two rounds of briefing in this case, two oral arguments, and 54 *amicus* briefs to help us carry out our obligation to decide the necessary constitutional questions according to law. We have also had the benefit of a comprehensive dissent that has helped ensure that the Court has considered all the relevant issues. This careful consideration convinces me that Congress violates the First Amendment when it decrees that some speakers may not engage in political speech at election time, when it matters most.

SUPREME COURT OF THE UNITED STATES

No. 08–205

CITIZENS UNITED, APPELLANT *v.* FEDERAL
ELECTION COMMISSION

ON APPEAL FROM THE UNITED STATES DISTRICT COURT FOR
THE DISTRICT OF COLUMBIA

[January 21, 2010]

JUSTICE SCALIA, with whom JUSTICE ALITO joins, and
with whom JUSTICE THOMAS joins in part, concurring.

I join the opinion of the Court.[1]

I write separately to address JUSTICE STEVENS' discussion of *"Original Understandings," post,* at 34 (opinion
concurring in part and dissenting in part) (hereinafter
referred to as the dissent). This section of the dissent
purports to show that today's decision is not supported by
the original understanding of the First Amendment. The
dissent attempts this demonstration, however, in splendid
isolation from the text of the First Amendment. It never
shows why "the freedom of speech" that was the right of
Englishmen did not include the freedom to speak in association with other individuals, including association in the
corporate form. To be sure, in 1791 (as now) corporations
could pursue only the objectives set forth in their charters;
but the dissent provides no evidence that their speech in
the pursuit of those objectives could be censored.

Instead of taking this straightforward approach to
determining the Amendment's meaning, the dissent em-
barks on a detailed exploration of the Framers' views
about the "role of corporations in society." *Post,* at 35.
The Framers didn't like corporations, the dissent con-

---

[1] JUSTICE THOMAS does not join Part IV of the Court's opinion.

cludes, and therefore it follows (as night the day) that corporations had no rights of free speech. Of course the Framers' personal affection or disaffection for corporations is relevant only insofar as it can be thought to be reflected in the understood meaning of the text they enacted—not, as the dissent suggests, as a freestanding substitute for that text. But the dissent's distortion of proper analysis is even worse than that. Though faced with a constitutional text that makes no distinction between types of speakers, the dissent feels no necessity to provide even an isolated statement from the founding era to the effect that corporations are *not* covered, but places the burden on petitioners to bring forward statements showing that they *are* ("there is not a scintilla of evidence to support the notion that anyone believed [the First Amendment] would preclude regulatory distinctions based on the corporate form," *post,* at 34–35).

Despite the corporation-hating quotations the dissent has dredged up, it is far from clear that by the end of the 18th century corporations were despised. If so, how came there to be so many of them? The dissent's statement that there were few business corporations during the eighteenth century—"only a few hundred during all of the 18th century"—is misleading. *Post,* at 35, n. 53. There were approximately 335 charters issued to business corporations in the United States by the end of the 18th century.[2] See 2 J. Davis, Essays in the Earlier History of American Corporations 24 (1917) (reprint 2006) (hereinafter Davis). This was a "considerable extension of corporate enterprise

---

[2] The dissent protests that 1791 rather than 1800 should be the relevant date, and that "[m]ore than half of the century's total business charters were issued between 1796 and 1800." *Post,* at 35, n. 53. I used 1800 only because the dissent did. But in any case, it is surely fanciful to think that a consensus of hostility towards corporations was transformed into general favor at some magical moment between 1791 and 1796.

in the field of business," Davis 8, and represented "unprecedented growth," *id.*, at 309. Moreover, what seems
like a small number by today's standards surely does not
indicate the relative importance of corporations when the
Nation was considerably smaller. As I have previously
noted, "[b]y the end of the eighteenth century the corporation was a familiar figure in American economic life."
McConnell v. *Federal Election Comm'n*, 540 U. S. 93, 256
(2003) (SCALIA, J., concurring in part, concurring in judgment in part, and dissenting in part) (quoting C. Cooke,
Corporation Trust and Company 92 (1951) (hereinafter
Cooke)).

Even if we thought it proper to apply the dissent's approach of excluding from First Amendment coverage what
the Founders disliked, and even if we agreed that the
Founders disliked founding-era corporations; modern
corporations might not qualify for exclusion. Most of the
Founders' resentment towards corporations was directed
at the state-granted monopoly privileges that individually
chartered corporations enjoyed.[3] Modern corporations do
not have such privileges, and would probably have been
favored by most of our enterprising Founders—excluding,
perhaps, Thomas Jefferson and others favoring perpetua-
tion of an agrarian society. Moreover, if the Founders'
specific intent with respect to corporations is what matters, why does the dissent ignore the Founders' views
about other legal entities that have more in common with
modern business corporations than the founding-era cor-

-----

[3] "[P]eople in 1800 identified corporations with franchised monopo-
lies." L. Friedman, A History of American Law 194 (2d ed. 1985)
(hereinafter Friedman). "The chief cause for the changed popular
attitude towards business corporations that marked the opening of the
nineteenth century was the elimination of their inherent monopolistic
character. This was accomplished primarily by an extension of the
principle of free incorporation under general laws." 1 W. Fletcher,
Cyclopedia of the Law of Corporations §2, p. 8 (rev. ed. 2006).

porations? At the time of the founding, religious, educational, and literary corporations were incorporated under general incorporation statutes, much as business corporations are today.[4] See Davis 16–17; R. Seavoy, Origins of the American Business Corporation, 1784–1855, p. 5 (1982); Cooke 94. There were also small unincorporated business associations, which some have argued were the "'true progenitors'" of today's business corporations. Friedman 200 (quoting S. Livermore, Early American Land Companies: Their Influence on Corporate Development 216 (1939)); see also Davis 33. Were all of these silently excluded from the protections of the First Amendment?

The lack of a textual exception for speech by corporations cannot be explained on the ground that such organizations did not exist or did not speak. To the contrary, colleges, towns and cities, religious institutions, and guilds had long been organized as corporations at common law and under the King's charter, see 1 W. Blackstone, Commentaries on the Laws of England 455–473 (1765); 1 S. Kyd, A Treatise on the Law of Corporations 1–32, 63 (1793) (reprinted 2006), and as I have discussed, the practice of incorporation only expanded in the United States. Both corporations and voluntary associations actively petitioned the Government and expressed their views in newspapers and pamphlets. For example: An antislavery Quaker corporation petitioned the First Congress, distributed pamphlets, and communicated through the press in 1790. W. diGiacomantonio, "For the Gratification of a Volunteering Society": Antislavery and Pressure Group

---

[4] At times (though not always) the dissent seems to exclude such non-"business corporations" from its denial of free speech rights. See *post*, at 37. Finding in a seemingly categorical text a distinction between the rights of business corporations and the rights of non-business corporations is even more imaginative than finding a distinction between the rights of *all* corporations and the rights of other associations.

Politics in the First Federal Congress, 15 J. Early Republic 169 (1995). The New York Sons of Liberty sent a circu-
lar to colonies farther south in 1766. P. Maier, From
Resistance to Revolution 79–80 (1972). And the Society
for the Relief and Instruction of Poor Germans circulated a
biweekly paper from 1755 to 1757. Adams, The Colonial
German-language Press and the American Revolution, in
The Press & the American Revolution 151, 161–162 (B.
Bailyn & J. Hench eds. 1980). The dissent offers no evidence—none whatever—that the First Amendment's
unqualified text was originally understood to exclude such
associational speech from its protection.[5]

---

[5]The best the dissent can come up with is that "[p]ostratification
practice" supports its reading of the First Amendment. *Post*, at 40,
n. 56. For this proposition, the dissent cites Justice White's statement
(in dissent) that "[t]he common law was generally interpreted as
prohibiting corporate political participation," *First Nat. Bank of Boston*
v. *Bellotti*, 435 U. S. 765, 819 (1978). The sole authority Justice White
cited for this proposition, *id.*, at 819, n. 14, was a law-review note that
made no such claim. To the contrary, it stated that the cases dealing
with the propriety of corporate political expenditures were "few." Note,
Corporate Political Affairs Programs, 70 Yale L. J. 821, 852 (1961).
More specifically, the note cites only two holdings to that effect, one by
a Federal District Court, and one by the Supreme Court of Montana.
Id., at 852, n. 197. Of course even if the common law was "generally
interpreted" to prohibit corporate political expenditures as ultra vires,
that would have nothing to do with whether political expenditures that
were authorized by a corporation's charter could constitutionally be
suppressed.

As additional "[p]ostratification practice," the dissent notes that the
Court "did not recognize *any* First Amendment protections for corporations until the middle part of the 20th century." *Post*, at 40, n. 56. But
it did that in *Grosjean* v. *American Press Co.*, 297 U. S. 233 (1936), a
case involving freedom of the press—which the dissent acknowledges
did cover corporations from the outset. The relative recency of that
first case is unsurprising. All of our First Amendment jurisprudence
was slow to develop. We did not consider application of the First
Amendment to speech restrictions other than prior restraints until
1919, see *Schenck* v. *United States*, 249 U. S. 47 (1919); we did not
invalidate a state law on First Amendment grounds until 1931, see

Historical evidence relating to the textually similar clause "the freedom of . . . the press" also provides no support for the proposition that the First Amendment excludes conduct of artificial legal entities from the scope of its protection. The freedom of "the press" was widely understood to protect the publishing activities of individual editors and printers. See *McIntyre* v. *Ohio Elections Comm'n,* 514 U. S. 334, 360 (1995) (THOMAS, J., concurring in judgment); see also *McConnell,* 540 U. S., at 252–253 (opinion of SCALIA, J.). But these individuals often acted through newspapers, which (much like corporations) had their own names, outlived the individuals who had founded them, could be bought and sold, were sometimes owned by more than one person, and were operated for profit. See generally F. Mott, American Journalism: A History of Newspapers in the United States Through 250 Years 3–164 (1941); J. Smith, Freedom's Fetters (1956). Their activities were not stripped of First Amendment protection simply because they were carried out under the banner of an artificial legal entity. And the notion which follows from the dissent's view, that modern newspapers, since they are incorporated, have free-speech rights only at the sufferance of Congress, boggles the mind.[6]

Stromberg v. *California,* 283 U. S. 359 (1931), and a federal law until 1965, see *Lamont* v. *Postmaster General,* 381 U. S. 301 (1965).

[6] The dissent seeks to avoid this conclusion (and to turn a liability into an asset) by interpreting the Freedom of the Press Clause to refer to the institutional press (thus demonstrating, according to the dissent, that the Founders "did draw distinctions—explicit distinctions—between types of 'speakers,' or speech outlets or forms"). *Post,* at 40 and n. 57. It is passing strange to interpret the phrase "the freedom of speech, or of the press" to mean, not everyone's right to speak or publish, but rather everyone's right to speak or the institutional press's right to publish. No one thought that is what it meant. Patriot Noah Webster's 1828 dictionary contains, under the word "press," the following entry:

"*Liberty of the press,* in civil policy, is the free right of publishing

In passing, the dissent also claims that the Court's conception of corruption is unhistorical. The Framers "would have been appalled," it says, by the evidence of corruption in the congressional findings supporting the Bipartisan Campaign Reform Act of 2002. *Post*, at 61. For this proposition, the dissent cites a law review article arguing that "corruption" was originally understood to include "moral decay" and even actions taken by citizens in pursuit of private rather than public ends. Teachout, The Anti-Corruption Principle, 94 Cornell L. Rev. 341, 373, 378 (2009). It is hard to see how this has anything to do with what sort of corruption can be combated by restrictions on political speech. Moreover, if speech can be prohibited because, in the view of the Government, it leads to "moral decay" or does not serve "public ends," then there is no limit to the Government's censorship power.

The dissent says that when the Framers "constitutionalized the right to free speech in the First Amendment, it was the free speech of individual Americans that they had in mind." *Post*, at 37. That is no doubt true. All the provisions of the Bill of Rights set forth the rights of individual men and women—not, for example, of trees or polar bears. But the individual person's right to speak includes the right to speak *in association with other individual persons*. Surely the dissent does not believe that speech

---

books, pamphlets, or papers without previous restraint; or the unrestrained right which every citizen enjoys of publishing his thoughts and opinions, subject only to punishment for publishing what is pernicious to morals or to the peace of the state." 2 American Dictionary of the English Language (1828) (reprinted 1970).

As the Court's opinion describes, *ante*, at 36, our jurisprudence agrees with Noah Webster and contradicts the dissent.

"The liberty of the press is not confined to newspapers and periodicals. It necessarily embraces pamphlets and leaflets. . . . The press in its historical connotation comprehends every sort of publication which affords a vehicle of information and opinion." *Lovell* v. *City of Griffin*, 303 U. S. 444, 452 (1938).

by the Republican Party or the Democratic Party can be censored because it is not the speech of "an individual American." It is the speech of many individual Americans, who have associated in a common cause, giving the leadership of the party the right to speak on their behalf. The association of individuals in a business corporation is no different—or at least it cannot be denied the right to speak on the simplistic ground that it is not "an individual American."[7]

But to return to, and summarize, my principal point, which is the conformity of today's opinion with the original meaning of the First Amendment. The Amendment is written in terms of "speech," not speakers. Its text offers no foothold for excluding any category of speaker, from

---

[7]The dissent says that "'speech'" refers to oral communications of human beings, and since corporations are not human beings they cannot speak. *Post*, at 37, n. 55. This is sophistry. The authorized spokesman of a corporation is a human being, who speaks on behalf of the human beings who have formed that association—just as the spokesman of an unincorporated association speaks on behalf of its members. The power to publish thoughts, no less than the power to speak thoughts, belongs only to human beings, but the dissent sees no problem with a corporation's enjoying the freedom of the press.

The same footnote asserts that "it has been 'claimed that the notion of institutional speech . . . did not exist in post-revolutionary America.'" This is quoted from a law-review article by a Bigelow Fellow at the University of Chicago (Fagundes, State Actors as First Amendment Speakers, 100 Nw. U. L. Rev. 1637, 1654 (2006)), which offers as the sole support for its statement a treatise dealing with government speech, M. Yudof, When Government Speaks 42–50 (1983). The cited pages of that treatise provide no support whatever for the statement—unless, as seems overwhelmingly likely, the "institutional speech" referred to was speech by the subject of the law-review article, governmental institutions.

The other authority cited in the footnote, a law-review article by a professor at Washington and Lee Law School, Bezanson, Institutional Speech, 80 Iowa L. Rev. 735, 775 (1995), in fact contradicts the dissent, in that it would accord free-speech protection to associations.

single individuals to partnerships of individuals, to unincorporated associations of individuals, to incorporated associations of individuals—and the dissent offers no evidence about the original meaning of the text to support any such exclusion. We are therefore simply left with the question whether the speech at issue in this case is "speech" covered by the First Amendment. No one says otherwise. A documentary film critical of a potential Presidential candidate is core political speech, and its nature as such does not change simply because it was funded by a corporation. Nor does the character of that funding produce any reduction whatever in the "inherent worth of the speech" and "its capacity for informing the public," *First Nat. Bank of Boston* v. *Bellotti*, 435 U. S. 765, 777 (1978). Indeed, to exclude or impede corporate speech is to muzzle the principal agents of the modern free economy. We should celebrate rather than condemn the addition of this speech to the public debate.

SUPREME COURT OF THE UNITED STATES

No. 08–205

CITIZENS UNITED, APPELLANT *v.* FEDERAL ELECTION COMMISSION

ON APPEAL FROM THE UNITED STATES DISTRICT COURT FOR THE DISTRICT OF COLUMBIA

[January 21, 2010]

JUSTICE STEVENS, with whom JUSTICE GINSBURG, JUSTICE BREYER, and JUSTICE SOTOMAYOR join, concurring in part and dissenting in part.

The real issue in this case concerns how, not if, the appellant may finance its electioneering. Citizens United is a wealthy nonprofit corporation that runs a political action committee (PAC) with millions of dollars in assets. Under the Bipartisan Campaign Reform Act of 2002 (BCRA), it could have used those assets to televise and promote *Hillary: The Movie* wherever and whenever it wanted to. It also could have spent unrestricted sums to broadcast *Hillary* at any time other than the 30 days before the last primary election. Neither Citizens United's nor any other corporation's speech has been "banned," *ante*, at 1. All that the parties dispute is whether Citizens United had a right to use the funds in its general treasury to pay for broadcasts during the 30-day period. The notion that the First Amendment dictates an affirmative answer to that question is, in my judgment, profoundly misguided. Even more misguided is the notion that the Court must rewrite the law relating to campaign expenditures by *for-profit* corporations and unions to decide this case.

The basic premise underlying the Court's ruling is its iteration, and constant reiteration, of the proposition that the First Amendment bars regulatory distinctions based on a speaker's identity, including its "identity" as a corporation. While that glittering generality has rhetorical appeal, it is not a correct statement of the law. Nor does it tell us when a corporation may engage in electioneering that some of its shareholders oppose. It does not even resolve the specific question whether Citizens United may be required to finance some of its messages with the money in its PAC. The conceit that corporations must be treated identically to natural persons in the political sphere is not only inaccurate but also inadequate to justify the Court's disposition of this case.

In the context of election to public office, the distinction between corporate and human speakers is significant. Although they make enormous contributions to our society, corporations are not actually members of it. They cannot vote or run for office. Because they may be managed and controlled by nonresidents, their interests may conflict in fundamental respects with the interests of eligible voters. The financial resources, legal structure, and instrumental orientation of corporations raise legitimate concerns about their role in the electoral process. Our lawmakers have a compelling constitutional basis, if not also a democratic duty, to take measures designed to guard against the potentially deleterious effects of corporate spending in local and national races.

The majority's approach to corporate electioneering marks a dramatic break from our past. Congress has placed special limitations on campaign spending by corporations ever since the passage of the Tillman Act in 1907, ch. 420, 34 Stat. 864. We have unanimously concluded that this "reflects a permissible assessment of the dangers posed by those entities to the electoral process," *FEC* v. *National Right to Work Comm.*, 459 U. S. 197, 209 (1982) *(NRWC)*, and have accepted the "legislative judgment that the special characteristics of the corporate structure require particularly careful regulation," *id.*, at 209–210. The

Court today rejects a century of history when it treats the distinction between corporate and individual campaign spending as an invidious novelty born of *Austin* v. *Michigan Chamber of Commerce*, 494 U. S. 652 (1990). Relying largely on individual dissenting opinions, the majority blazes through our precedents, overruling or disavowing a body of case law including *FEC* v. *Wisconsin Right to Life, Inc.*, 551 U. S. 449 (2007) *(WRTL)*, *McConnell* v. *FEC*, 540 U. S. 93 (2003), *FEC* v. *Beaumont*, 539 U. S. 146 (2003), *FEC* v. *Massachusetts Citizens for Life, Inc.*, 479 U. S. 238 (1986) *(MCFL)*, *NRWC*, 459 U. S. 197, and *California Medical Assn.* v. *FEC*, 453 U. S. 182 (1981).

In his landmark concurrence in *Ashwander* v. *TVA*, 297 U. S. 288, 346 (1936), Justice Brandeis stressed the importance of adhering to rules the Court has "developed . . . for its own governance" when deciding constitutional questions. Because departures from those rules always enhance the risk of error, I shall review the background of this case in some detail before explaining why the Court's analysis rests on a faulty understanding of *Austin* and *McConnell* and of our campaign finance jurisprudence more generally.[1] I regret the length of what follows, but the importance and novelty of the Court's opinion require a full response. Although I concur in the Court's decision to sustain BCRA's disclosure provisions and join Part IV of its opinion, I emphatically dissent from its principal holding.

---

[1] Specifically, Part I, *infra*, at 4–17, addresses the procedural history of the case and the narrower grounds of decision the majority has bypassed. Part II, *infra*, at 17–23, addresses *stare decisis*. Part III, *infra*, at 23–56, addresses the Court's assumptions that BCRA "bans" corporate speech, that identity-based distinctions may not be drawn in the political realm, and that *Austin* and *McConnell* were outliers in our First Amendment tradition. Part IV, *infra*, at 56–89, addresses the Court's treatment of the anticorruption, antidistortion, and shareholder protection rationales for regulating corporate electioneering.

I

The Court's ruling threatens to undermine the integrity of elected institutions across the Nation. The path it has taken to reach its outcome will, I fear, do damage to this institution. Before turning to the question whether to overrule *Austin* and part of *McConnell*, it is important to explain why the Court should not be deciding that question.

Scope of the Case

The first reason is that the question was not properly brought before us. In declaring §203 of BCRA facially unconstitutional on the ground that corporations' electoral expenditures may not be regulated any more stringently than those of individuals, the majority decides this case on a basis relinquished below, not included in the questions presented to us by the litigants, and argued here only in response to the Court's invitation. This procedure is unusual and inadvisable for a court.[2] Our colleagues' suggestion that "we are asked to reconsider *Austin* and, in effect, *McConnell*," *ante*, at 1, would be more accurate if rephrased to state that "we have asked ourselves" to reconsider those cases.

In the District Court, Citizens United initially raised a facial challenge to the constitutionality of §203. App. 23a–24a. In its motion for summary judgment, however, Citi-

---

[2] See *Yee* v. *Escondido*, 503 U. S. 519, 535 (1992) ("[U]nder this Court's Rule 14.1(a), only questions set forth in the petition, or fairly included therein, will be considered by the Court" (internal quotation marks and alteration omitted)); *Wood* v. *Allen*, *ante*, at __ (slip op., at 13) ("[T]he fact that petitioner discussed [an] issue in the text of his petition for certiorari does not bring it before us. Rule 14.1(a) requires that a subsidiary question be fairly included in the *question presented* for our review" (internal quotation marks and brackets omitted)); *Cooper Industries, Inc.* v. *Aviall Services, Inc.*, 543 U. S. 157, 168–169 (2004) ("We ordinarily do not decide in the first instance issues not decided below" (internal quotation marks omitted)).

zens United expressly abandoned its facial challenge, 1:07–cv–2240–RCL–RWR, Docket Entry No. 52, pp. 1–2 (May 16, 2008), and the parties stipulated to the dismissal of that claim, *id.*, Nos. 53 (May 22, 2008), 54 (May 23, 2008), App. 6a. The District Court therefore resolved the case on alternative grounds,[3] and in its jurisdictional statement to this Court, Citizens United properly advised us that it was raising only "an as-applied challenge to the constitutionality of . . . BCRA §203." Juris. Statement 5. The jurisdictional statement never so much as cited *Austin*, the key case the majority today overrules. And not one of the questions presented suggested that Citizens United was surreptitiously raising the facial challenge to §203 that it previously agreed to dismiss. In fact, not one of those questions raised an issue based on Citizens United's corporate status. Juris. Statement (i). Moreover, even in its merits briefing, when Citizens United injected its request to overrule *Austin*, it never sought a declaration that §203 was facially unconstitutional as to all corporations and unions; instead it argued only that the statute could not be applied to it because it was "funded overwhelmingly by individuals." Brief for Appellant 29; see also *id.,* at 10, 12, 16, 28 (affirming "as applied" character

---

[3] The majority states that, in denying Citizens United's motion for a preliminary injunction, the District Court "addressed" the facial validity of BCRA §203. *Ante,* at 13. That is true, in the narrow sense that the court observed the issue was foreclosed by *McConnell* v. *FEC*, 540 U. S. 93 (2003). See 530 F. Supp. 2d 274, 278 (DC 2008) *(per curiam)*. Yet as explained above, Citizens United subsequently dismissed its facial challenge, so that by the time the District Court granted the Federal Election Commission's (FEC) motion for summary judgment, App. 261a–262a, any question about statutory validity had dropped out of the case. That latter ruling by the District Court was the "final decision" from which Citizens United appealed to this Court under BCRA §403(a)(3). As regards the lower court decision that has come before us, the claim that §203 is facially unconstitutional was neither pressed nor passed upon in any form.

of challenge to §203); Tr. of Oral Arg. 4–9 (Mar. 24, 2009) (counsel for Citizens United conceding that §203 could be applied to General Motors); *id.,* at 55 (counsel for Citizens United stating that "we accept the Court's decision in *Wisconsin Right to Life*").

"'It is only in exceptional cases coming here from the federal courts that questions not pressed or passed upon below are reviewed,'" *Youakim* v. *Miller,* 425 U. S. 231, 234 (1976) *(per curiam)* (quoting *Duignan* v. *United States,* 274 U. S. 195, 200 (1927)), and it is "only in the most exceptional cases" that we will consider issues outside the questions presented, *Stone* v. *Powell,* 428 U. S. 465, 481, n. 15 (1976). The appellant in this case did not so much as assert an exceptional circumstance, and one searches the majority opinion in vain for the mention of any. That is unsurprising, for none exists.

Setting the case for reargument was a constructive step, but it did not cure this fundamental problem. Essentially, five Justices were unhappy with the limited nature of the case before us, so they changed the case to give themselves an opportunity to change the law.

As-Applied and Facial Challenges

This Court has repeatedly emphasized in recent years that "[f]acial challenges are disfavored." *Washington State Grange* v. *Washington State Republican Party,* 552 U. S. 442, 450 (2008); see also *Ayotte* v. *Planned Parenthood of Northern New Eng.,* 546 U. S. 320, 329 (2006) ("[T]he 'normal rule' is that 'partial, rather than facial, invalidation is the required course,' such that a 'statute may . . . be declared invalid to the extent that it reaches too far, but otherwise left intact'" (quoting *Brockett* v. *Spokane Arcades, Inc.,* 472 U. S. 491, 504 (1985); alteration in original)). By declaring §203 facially unconstitutional, our colleagues have turned an as-applied challenge into a facial challenge, in defiance of this principle.

This is not merely a technical defect in the Court's decision. The unnecessary resort to a facial inquiry "run[s] contrary to the fundamental principle of judicial restraint that courts should neither anticipate a question of constitutional law in advance of the necessity of deciding it nor formulate a rule of constitutional law broader than is required by the precise facts to which it is to be applied." *Washington State Grange*, 552 U. S., at 450 (internal quotation marks omitted). Scanting that principle "threaten[s] to short circuit the democratic process by preventing laws embodying the will of the people from being implemented in a manner consistent with the Constitution." *Id.,* at 451. These concerns are heightened when judges overrule settled doctrine upon which the legislature has relied. The Court operates with a sledge hammer rather than a scalpel when it strikes down one of Congress' most significant efforts to regulate the role that corporations and unions play in electoral politics. It compounds the offense by implicitly striking down a great many state laws as well.

The problem goes still deeper, for the Court does all of this on the basis of pure speculation. Had Citizens United maintained a facial challenge, and thus argued that there are virtually no circumstances in which BCRA §203 can be applied constitutionally, the parties could have developed, through the normal process of litigation, a record about the *actual* effects of §203, its actual burdens and its actual benefits, on *all* manner of corporations and unions.[4]

---

[4] Shortly before Citizens United mooted the issue by abandoning its facial challenge, the Government advised the District Court that it "require[d] time to develop a factual record regarding [the] facial challenge." 1:07–cv–2240–RCL–RWR, Docket Entry No. 47, p. 4 (Mar. 26, 2008). By reinstating a claim that Citizens United abandoned, the Court gives it a perverse litigating advantage over its adversary, which was deprived of the opportunity to gather and present information necessary to its rebuttal.

"Claims of facial invalidity often rest on speculation," and consequently "raise the risk of premature interpretation of statutes on the basis of factually barebones records." *Id.,* at 450 (internal quotation marks omitted). In this case, the record is not simply incomplete or unsatisfactory; it is nonexistent. Congress crafted BCRA in response to a virtual mountain of research on the corruption that previous legislation had failed to avert. The Court now negates Congress' efforts without a shred of evidence on how §203 or its state-law counterparts have been affecting any entity other than Citizens United.[5]

Faced with this gaping empirical hole, the majority throws up its hands. Were we to confine our inquiry to Citizens United's as-applied challenge, it protests, we would commence an "extended" process of "draw[ing], and then redraw[ing], constitutional lines based on the particular media or technology used to disseminate political speech from a particular speaker." *Ante,* at 9. While tacitly acknowledging that some applications of §203 might be found constitutional, the majority thus posits a future in which novel First Amendment standards must

---

[5] In fact, we do not even have a good evidentiary record of how §203 has been affecting Citizens United, which never submitted to the District Court the details of *Hillary*'s funding or its own finances. We likewise have no evidence of how §203 and comparable state laws were expected to affect corporations and unions in the future.

It is true, as the majority points out, that the *McConnell* Court evaluated the facial validity of §203 in light of an extensive record. See *ante,* at 15. But that record is not before us in this case. And in any event, the majority's argument for striking down §203 depends on its contention that the statute has proved too "chilling" in practice—and in particular on the contention that the controlling opinion in *WRTL,* 551 U. S. 449 (2007), failed to bring sufficient clarity and "breathing space" to this area of law. See *ante,* at 12, 16–20. We have no record with which to assess that claim. The Court complains at length about the burdens of complying with §203, but we have no meaningful evidence to show how regulated corporations and unions have experienced its restrictions.

be devised on an ad hoc basis, and then leaps from this unfounded prediction to the unfounded conclusion that such complexity counsels the abandonment of all normal restraint. Yet it is a pervasive feature of regulatory systems that unanticipated events, such as new technologies, may raise some unanticipated difficulties at the margins. The fluid nature of electioneering communications does not make this case special. The fact that a Court can hypothesize situations in which a statute might, at some point down the line, pose some unforeseen as-applied problems, does not come close to meeting the standard for a facial challenge.[6]

The majority proposes several other justifications for the sweep of its ruling. It suggests that a facial ruling is necessary because, if the Court were to continue on its normal course of resolving as-applied challenges as they present themselves, that process would itself run afoul of the First Amendment. See, *e.g., ante,* at 9 (as-applied review process "would raise questions as to the courts' own lawful authority"); *ibid.* ("Courts, too, are bound by the First Amendment"). This suggestion is perplexing. Our colleagues elsewhere trumpet "our duty 'to say what the law is,'" even when our predecessors on the bench and our counterparts in Congress have interpreted the law differ-

---

[6] Our cases recognize a "type of facial challenge in the First Amendment context under which a law may be overturned as impermissibly overbroad because a substantial number of its applications are unconstitutional." *Washington State Grange* v. *Washington State Republican Party,* 552 U. S. 442, 449, n. 6 (2008) (internal quotation marks omitted). Citizens United has not made an overbreadth argument, and "[w]e generally do not apply the strong medicine of overbreadth analysis where the parties fail to describe the instances of arguable overbreadth of the contested law," *ibid.* (internal quotation marks omitted). If our colleagues nonetheless concluded that §203's fatal flaw is that it affects too much protected speech, they should have invalidated it for overbreadth and given guidance as to which applications are permissible, so that Congress could go about repairing the error.

ently. *Ante,* at 49 (quoting *Marbury* v. *Madison,* 1 Cranch 137, 177 (1803)). We do not typically say what the law *is not* as a hedge against future judicial error. The possibility that later courts will misapply a constitutional provision does not give us a basis for pretermitting litigation relating to that provision.[7]

The majority suggests that a facial ruling is necessary because anything less would chill too much protected speech. See *ante,* at 9–10, 12, 16–20. In addition to begging the question what types of corporate spending are constitutionally protected and to what extent, this claim rests on the assertion that some significant number of corporations have been cowed into quiescence by FEC "'censor[ship].'" *Ante,* at 18–19. That assertion is unsubstantiated, and it is hard to square with practical experience. It is particularly hard to square with the legal landscape following *WRTL,* which held that a corporate communication could be regulated under §203 only if it was "susceptible of *no* reasonable interpretation other than as an appeal to vote for or against a specific candidate." 551 U. S., at 470 (opinion of ROBERTS, C. J.) (emphasis added). The whole point of this test was to make §203 as simple and speech-protective as possible. The Court does not explain how, in the span of a single election cycle, it has determined THE CHIEF JUSTICE's project to be

---

[7] Also perplexing is the majority's attempt to pass blame to the Government for its litigating position. By "hold[ing] out the possibility of ruling for Citizens United on a narrow ground yet refrain[ing] from adopting that position," the majority says, the Government has caused "added uncertainty [that] demonstrates the necessity to address the question of statutory validity." *Ante,* at 17. Our colleagues have apparently never heard of an alternative argument. Like every litigant, the Government would prefer to win its case outright; failing that, it would prefer to lose on a narrow ground. The fact that there are numerous different ways this case could be decided, and that the Government acknowledges as much, does not demonstrate anything about the propriety of a facial ruling.

a failure. In this respect, too, the majority's critique of line-drawing collapses into a critique of the as-applied review method generally.[8]

The majority suggests that, even though it expressly dismissed its facial challenge, Citizens United nevertheless preserved it—not as a freestanding "claim," but as a potential argument in support of "a claim that the FEC has violated its First Amendment right to free speech." *Ante*, at 13; see also *ante*, at 4 (ROBERTS, C. J., concurring) (describing Citizens United's claim as: "[T]he Act violates the First Amendment"). By this novel logic, virtually any submission could be reconceptualized as "a claim that the Government has violated my rights," and it would then be available to the Court to entertain any conceivable issue that might be relevant to that claim's disposition. Not only the as-applied/facial distinction, but the basic relationship between litigants and courts, would be upended if the latter had free rein to construe the former's claims at such high levels of generality. There would be no need for plaintiffs to argue their case; they could just cite the constitutional provisions they think relevant, and leave the rest to us.[9]

---

[8] The majority's "chilling" argument is particularly inapposite with respect to 2 U. S. C. §441b's longstanding restriction on the use of corporate general treasury funds for express advocacy. If there was ever any significant uncertainty about what counts as the functional equivalent of express advocacy, there has been little doubt about what counts as express advocacy since the "magic words" test of *Buckley* v. *Valeo*, 424 U. S. 1, 44, n. 52 (1976) *(per curiam)*. Yet even though Citizens United's briefs never once mention §441b's restriction on express advocacy; even though this restriction does not generate chilling concerns; and even though no one has suggested that *Hillary* counts as express advocacy; the majority nonetheless reaches out to opine that this statutory provision is "invalid" as well. *Ante*, at 50.

[9] The majority adds that the distinction between facial and as-applied challenges does not have "some automatic effect" that mechanically controls the judicial task. *Ante*, at 14. I agree, but it does not follow that in any given case we should ignore the distinction, much less

Finally, the majority suggests that though the scope of Citizens United's claim may be narrow, a facial ruling is necessary as a matter of remedy. Relying on a law review article, it asserts that Citizens United's dismissal of the facial challenge does not prevent us "'from making broader pronouncements of invalidity in properly "as-applied" cases.'" *Ante,* at 14 (quoting Fallon, As-Applied and Facial Challenges and Third-Party Standing, 113 Harv. L. Rev. 1321, 1339 (2000) (hereinafter Fallon)); accord, *ante,* at 5 (opinion of ROBERTS, C. J.) ("Regardless whether we label Citizens United's claim a 'facial' or 'as-applied' challenge, the consequences of the Court's decision are the same"). The majority is on firmer conceptual ground here. Yet even if one accepts this part of Professor Fallon's thesis, one must proceed to ask *which* as-applied challenges, if successful, will "properly" invite or entail invalidation of the underlying statute.[10] The paradigmatic case is a judicial determination that the legislature acted with an impermissible purpose in enacting a provision, as this carries the necessary implication that all future as-applied challenges to the provision must prevail. See Fallon 1339–1340.

Citizens United's as-applied challenge was not of this sort. Until this Court ordered reargument, its contention was that BCRA §203 could not lawfully be applied to a

---

invert it.

[10] Professor Fallon proposes an intricate answer to this question that the majority ignores. Fallon 1327–1359. It bears mention that our colleagues have previously cited Professor Fallon's article for the exact opposite point from the one they wish to make today. In *Gonzales* v. *Carhart,* 550 U. S. 124 (2007), the Court explained that "[i]t is neither our obligation nor within our traditional institutional role to resolve questions of constitutionality with respect to each potential situation that might develop," and "[f]or this reason, '[a]s-applied challenges are the basic building blocks of constitutional adjudication.'" *Id.,* at 168 (opinion for the Court by KENNEDY, J.) (quoting Fallon 1328 (second alteration in original)).

feature-length video-on-demand film (such as *Hillary*) or to a nonprofit corporation exempt from taxation under 26 U. S. C. §501(c)(4)[11] and funded overwhelmingly by individuals (such as itself). See Brief for Appellant 16–41. Success on either of these claims would not necessarily carry any implications for the validity of §203 as applied to other types of broadcasts, other types of corporations, or unions. It certainly would not invalidate the statute as applied to a large for-profit corporation. See Tr. of Oral Arg. 8, 4 (Mar. 24, 2009) (counsel for Citizens United emphasizing that appellant is "a small, nonprofit organization, which is very much like [an *MCFL* corporation]," and affirming that its argument "definitely would not be the same" if *Hillary* were distributed by General Motors).[12] There is no legitimate basis for resurrecting a facial chal-

---

[11] Internal Revenue Code section 501(c)(4) applies, *inter alia*, to nonprofit organizations "operated exclusively for the promotion of social welfare, . . . the net earnings of which are devoted exclusively to charitable, educational, or recreational purposes."

[12] THE CHIEF JUSTICE is therefore much too quick when he suggests that, "[e]ven if considered in as-applied terms, a holding in this case that the Act may not be applied to Citizens United—because corporations as well as individuals enjoy the pertinent First Amendment rights—would mean that any other corporation raising the same challenge would also win." *Ante*, at 4 (concurring opinion). That conclusion would only follow if the Court were to ignore Citizens United's plausible as-applied arguments and instead take the implausible position that *all* corporations and *all* types of expenditures enjoy the same First Amendment protections, which *always* trump the interests in regulation. At times, the majority appears to endorse this extreme view. At other times, however, it appears to suggest that nonprofit corporations have a better claim to First Amendment protection than for-profit corporations, see *ante*, at 20, 39, "advocacy" organizations have a better claim than other nonprofits, *ante*, at 20, domestic corporations have a better claim than foreign corporations, *ante*, at 46–47, small corporations have a better claim than large corporations, *ante*, at 38–40, and printed matter has a better claim than broadcast communications, *ante*, at 33. The majority never uses a multinational business corporation in its hypotheticals.

lenge that dropped out of this case 20 months ago.

Narrower Grounds

It is all the more distressing that our colleagues have manufactured a facial challenge, because the parties have advanced numerous ways to resolve the case that would facilitate electioneering by nonprofit advocacy corporations such as Citizens United, without toppling statutes and precedents. Which is to say, the majority has transgressed yet another "cardinal" principle of the judicial process: "[I]f it is not necessary to decide more, it is necessary not to decide more," *PDK Labs., Inc.* v. *Drug Enforcement Admin.*, 362 F. 3d 786, 799 (CADC 2004) (Roberts, J., concurring in part and concurring in judgment).

Consider just three of the narrower grounds of decision that the majority has bypassed. First, the Court could have ruled, on statutory grounds, that a feature-length film distributed through video-on-demand does not qualify as an "electioneering communication" under §203 of BCRA, 2 U. S. C. §441b. BCRA defines that term to encompass certain communications transmitted by "broadcast, cable, or satellite." §434(f)(3)(A). When Congress was developing BCRA, the video-on-demand medium was still in its infancy, and legislators were focused on a very different sort of programming: short advertisements run on television or radio. See *McConnell*, 540 U. S., at 207. The sponsors of BCRA acknowledge that the FEC's implementing regulations do not clearly apply to video-on-demand transmissions. See Brief for Senator John McCain et al. as *Amici Curiae* 17–19. In light of this ambiguity, the distinctive characteristics of video-on-demand, and "[t]he elementary rule . . . that every reasonable construction must be resorted to, in order to save a statute from unconstitutionality," *Hooper* v. *California*, 155 U. S. 648, 657 (1895), the Court could have reasonably ruled that §203 does not apply to *Hillary*.[13]

Second, the Court could have expanded the *MCFL* exemption to cover §501(c)(4) nonprofits that accept only a *de minimis* amount of money from for-profit corporations. Citizens United professes to be such a group: Its brief says it "is funded predominantly by donations from individuals who support [its] ideological message." Brief for Appellant 5. Numerous Courts of Appeal have held that *de minimis* business support does not, in itself, remove an otherwise qualifying organization from the ambit of *MCFL*.[14] This Court could have simply followed their lead.[15]

Finally, let us not forget Citizens United's as-applied constitutional challenge. Precisely because Citizens

---

[13] The Court entirely ignores this statutory argument. It concludes that §203 applies to *Hillary* on the basis of the film's content, *ante*, at 7–8, without considering the possibility that §203 does not apply to video-on-demand transmissions generally.

[14] See *Colorado Right to Life Comm., Inc. v. Coffman*, 498 F. 3d 1137, 1148 (CA10 2007) (adopting this rule and noting that "every other circuit to have addressed this issue" has done likewise); Brief for Independent Sector as *Amicus Curiae* 10–11 (collecting cases). The Court rejects this solution in part because the Government "merely suggest[s] it" and "does not say that it agrees with the interpretation." *Ante*, at 11. Our colleagues would thus punish a defendant for showing insufficient excitement about a ground it has advanced, at the same time that they decide the case on a ground the plaintiff expressly abandoned. The Court also protests that a *de minimis* standard would "requir[e] intricate case-by-case determinations." *Ante*, at 12. But *de minimis* tests need not be intricate at all. A test that granted *MCFL* status to §501(c)(4) organizations if they received less than a fixed dollar amount of business donations in the previous year, or if such donations represent less than a fixed percentage of their total assets, would be perfectly easy to understand and administer.

[15] Another bypassed ground, not briefed by the parties, would have been to revive the Snowe-Jeffords Amendment in BCRA §203(c), allowing certain nonprofit corporations to pay for electioneering communications with general treasury funds, to the extent they can trace the payments to individual contributions. See Brief for National Rifle Association as *Amicus Curiae* 5–15 (arguing forcefully that Congress intended this result).

United looks so much like the *MCFL* organizations we have exempted from regulation, while a feature-length video-on-demand film looks so unlike the types of electoral advocacy Congress has found deserving of regulation, this challenge is a substantial one. As the appellant's own arguments show, the Court could have easily limited the breadth of its constitutional holding had it declined to adopt the novel notion that speakers and speech acts must always be treated identically—and always spared expenditures restrictions—in the political realm. Yet the Court nonetheless turns its back on the as-applied review process that has been a staple of campaign finance litigation since *Buckley* v. *Valeo*, 424 U. S. 1 (1976) *(per curiam)*, and that was affirmed and expanded just two Terms ago in *WRTL*, 551 U. S. 449.

This brief tour of alternative grounds on which the case could have been decided is not meant to show that any of these grounds is ideal, though each is perfectly "valid," *ante*, at 12 (majority opinion).[16] It is meant to show that there were principled, narrower paths that a Court that was serious about judicial restraint could have taken. There was also the straightforward path: applying *Austin* and *McConnell*, just as the District Court did in holding

---

[16] THE CHIEF JUSTICE finds our discussion of these narrower solutions "quite perplexing" because we suggest that the Court should "latch on to one of them in order to avoid reaching the broader constitutional question," without doing the same ourselves. *Ante*, at 3. There is nothing perplexing about the matter, because we are not similarly situated to our colleagues in the majority. We do not share their view of the First Amendment. Our reading of the Constitution would not lead us to strike down any statutes or overturn any precedents in this case, and we therefore have no occasion to practice constitutional avoidance or to vindicate Citizens United's as-applied challenge. Each of the arguments made above is surely at least as strong as the statutory argument the Court accepted in last year's Voting Rights Act case, *Northwest Austin Municipal Util. Dist. No. One* v. *Holder*, 557 U. S. __ (2009).

that the funding of Citizens United's film can be regulated under them. The only thing preventing the majority from affirming the District Court, or adopting a narrower ground that would retain *Austin*, is its disdain for *Austin*.

II

The final principle of judicial process that the majority violates is the most transparent: *stare decisis*. I am not an absolutist when it comes to *stare decisis*, in the campaign finance area or in any other. No one is. But if this principle is to do any meaningful work in supporting the rule of law, it must at least demand a significant justification, beyond the preferences of five Justices, for overturning settled doctrine. "[A] decision to overrule should rest on some special reason over and above the belief that a prior case was wrongly decided." *Planned Parenthood of Southeastern Pa.* v. *Casey*, 505 U. S. 833, 864 (1992). No such justification exists in this case, and to the contrary there are powerful prudential reasons to keep faith with our precedents.[17]

The Court's central argument for why *stare decisis* ought to be trumped is that it does not like *Austin*. The opinion "was not well reasoned," our colleagues assert, and it conflicts with First Amendment principles. *Ante*, at 47–48. This, of course, is the Court's merits argument, the many defects in which we will soon consider. I am perfectly willing to concede that if one of our precedents were dead wrong in its reasoning or irreconcilable with the rest of our doctrine, there would be a compelling basis for revisiting it. But neither is true of *Austin*, as I explain at length in Parts III and IV, *infra*, at 23–89, and restating a merits argument with additional vigor does not give it

---

[17] I will have more to say shortly about the merits—about why *Austin* and *McConnell* are not doctrinal outliers, as the Court contends, and why their logic is not only defensible but also compelling. For present purposes, I limit the discussion to *stare-decisis*-specific considerations.

extra weight in the *stare decisis* calculus.

Perhaps in recognition of this point, the Court supplements its merits case with a smattering of assertions. The Court proclaims that "*Austin* is undermined by experience since its announcement." *Ante*, at 48. This is a curious claim to make in a case that lacks a developed record. The majority has no empirical evidence with which to substantiate the claim; we just have its *ipse dixit* that the real world has not been kind to *Austin*. Nor does the majority bother to specify in what sense *Austin* has been "undermined." Instead it treats the reader to a string of non sequiturs: "Our Nation's speech dynamic is changing," *ante*, at 48; "[s]peakers have become adept at presenting citizens with sound bites, talking points, and scripted messages," *ibid.;* "[c]orporations . . . do not have monolithic views," *ibid.* How any of these ruminations weakens the force of *stare decisis*, escapes my comprehension.[18]

The majority also contends that the Government's hesitation to rely on *Austin*'s antidistortion rationale "diminishe[s]" "the principle of adhering to that precedent." *Ante*, at 48; see also *ante*, at 11 (opinion of ROBERTS, C. J.) (Government's litigating position is "most importan[t]"

---

[18] THE CHIEF JUSTICE suggests that *Austin* has been undermined by subsequent dissenting opinions. *Ante*, at 9. Under this view, it appears that the more times the Court stands by a precedent in the face of requests to overrule it, the weaker that precedent becomes. THE CHIEF JUSTICE further suggests that *Austin* "is uniquely destabilizing because it threatens to subvert our Court's decisions even outside" its particular facts, as when we applied its reasoning in *McConnell*. *Ante*, at 9. Once again, the theory seems to be that the more we utilize a precedent, the more we call it into question. For those who believe *Austin* was correctly decided—as the Federal Government and the States have long believed, as the majority of Justices to have served on the Court since *Austin* have believed, and as we continue to believe—there is nothing "destabilizing" about the prospect of its continued application. It is gutting campaign finance laws across the country, as the Court does today, that will be destabilizing.

factor undermining *Austin*). Why it diminishes the value of *stare decisis* is left unexplained. We have never thought fit to overrule a precedent because a litigant has taken any particular tack. Nor should we. Our decisions can often be defended on multiple grounds, and a litigant may have strategic or case-specific reasons for emphasizing only a subset of them. Members of the public, moreover, often rely on our bottom-line holdings far more than our precise legal arguments; surely this is true for the legislatures that have been regulating corporate electioneering since *Austin*. The task of evaluating the continued viability of precedents falls to this Court, not to the parties.[19]

Although the majority opinion spends several pages making these surprising arguments, it says almost nothing about the standard considerations we have used to determine *stare decisis* value, such as the antiquity of the precedent, the workability of its legal rule, and the reliance interests at stake. It is also conspicuously silent about *McConnell*, even though the *McConnell* Court's decision to uphold BCRA §203 relied not only on the antidistortion logic of *Austin* but also on the statute's historical pedigree, see, *e.g.*, 540 U. S., at 115–132, 223–224, and the need to preserve the integrity of federal campaigns, see *id.*, at 126–129, 205–208, and n. 88.

We have recognized that "*[s]tare decisis* has special force when legislators or citizens 'have acted in reliance on a previous decision, for in this instance overruling the deci-

---

[19] Additionally, the majority cites some recent scholarship challenging the historical account of campaign finance law given in *United States* v. *Automobile Workers*, 352 U. S. 567 (1957). *Ante*, at 48. *Austin* did not so much as allude to this historical account, much less rely on it. Even if the scholarship cited by the majority is correct that certain campaign finance reforms were less deliberate or less benignly motivated than *Automobile Workers* suggested, the point remains that this body of law has played a significant and broadly accepted role in American political life for decades upon decades.

sion would dislodge settled rights and expectations or require an extensive legislative response.'" *Hubbard* v. *United States,* 514 U. S. 695, 714 (1995) (quoting *Hilton* v. *South Carolina Public Railways Comm'n,* 502 U. S. 197, 202 (1991)). *Stare decisis* protects not only personal rights involving property or contract but also the ability of the elected branches to shape their laws in an effective and coherent fashion.   Today's decision takes away a power that we have long permitted these branches to exercise. State legislatures have relied on their authority to regulate corporate electioneering, confirmed in *Austin,* for more than a century.[20]   The Federal Congress has relied on this authority for a comparable stretch of time, and it specifically relied on *Austin* throughout the years it spent developing and debating BCRA.   The total record it compiled was *100,000 pages* long.[21]   Pulling out the rug beneath Congress after affirming the constitutionality of §203 six years ago shows great disrespect for a coequal branch.

By removing one of its central components, today's ruling makes a hash out of BCRA's "delicate and interconnected regulatory scheme." *McConnell,* 540 U. S., at 172. Consider just one example of the distortions that will follow: Political parties are barred under BCRA from soliciting or spending "soft money," funds that are not subject to the statute's disclosure requirements or its source and amount limitations.   2 U. S. C. §441i; *McConnell,* 540 U. S., at 122–126.   Going forward, corporations and unions will be free to spend as much general treasury money as they wish on ads that support or attack specific

---

[20] See Brief for State of Montana et al. as *Amici Curiae* 5–13; see also Supp. Brief for Senator John McCain et al. as *Amici Curiae* 1a–8a (listing 24 States that presently limit or prohibit independent electioneering expenditures from corporate general treasuries).

[21] Magleby, The Importance of the Record in *McConnell v. FEC,* 3 Election L. J. 285 (2004).

candidates, whereas national parties will not be able to spend a dime of soft money on ads of any kind. The Court's ruling thus dramatically enhances the role of corporations and unions—and the narrow interests they represent—vis-à-vis the role of political parties—and the broad coalitions they represent—in determining who will hold public office.[22]

Beyond the reliance interests at stake, the other *stare decisis* factors also cut against the Court. Considerations of antiquity are significant for similar reasons. *McConnell* is only six years old, but *Austin* has been on the books for two decades, and many of the statutes called into question by today's opinion have been on the books for a half-century or more. The Court points to no intervening change in circumstances that warrants revisiting *Austin*. Certainly nothing relevant has changed since we decided *WRTL* two Terms ago. And the Court gives no reason to think that *Austin* and *McConnell* are unworkable.

In fact, no one has argued to us that *Austin*'s rule has proved impracticable, and not a single for-profit corporation, union, or State has asked us to overrule it. Quite to the contrary, leading groups representing the business community,[23] organized labor,[24] and the nonprofit sector,[25] together with more than half of the States,[26] urge that we

---

[22] To be sure, the majority may respond that Congress can correct the imbalance by removing BCRA's soft-money limits. Cf. Tr. of Oral Arg. 24 (Sept. 9, 2009) (query of KENNEDY, J.). But this is no response to any legislature that takes campaign finance regulation seriously. It merely illustrates the breadth of the majority's deregulatory vision.

[23] See Brief for Committee for Economic Development as *Amicus Curiae;* Brief for American Independent Business Alliance as *Amicus Curiae.* But see Supp. Brief for Chamber of Commerce of the United States of America as *Amicus Curiae.*

[24] See Brief for American Federation of Labor and Congress of Industrial Organizations as *Amicus Curiae* 3, 9.

[25] See Brief for Independent Sector as *Amicus Curiae* 16–20.

[26] See Brief for State of Montana et al. as *Amici Curiae.*

preserve *Austin.* As for *McConnell,* the portions of BCRA it upheld may be prolix, but all three branches of Government have worked to make §203 as user-friendly as possible. For instance, Congress established a special mechanism for expedited review of constitutional challenges, see note following 2 U. S. C. §437h; the FEC has established a standardized process, with clearly defined safe harbors, for corporations to claim that a particular electioneering communication is permissible under *WRTL,* see 11 CFR §114.15 (2009);[27] and, as noted above, THE CHIEF JUSTICE crafted his controlling opinion in *WRTL* with the express goal of maximizing clarity and administrability, 551 U. S., at 469–470, 473–474. The case for *stare decisis* may be bolstered, we have said, when subsequent rulings "have reduced the impact" of a precedent "while reaffirming the decision's core ruling." *Dickerson* v. *United States,* 530 U. S. 428, 443 (2000).[28]

In the end, the Court's rejection of *Austin* and *McCon-*

---

[27] The FEC established this process following the Court's June 2007 decision in that case, 551 U. S. 449. In the brief interval between the establishment of this process and the 2008 election, corporations and unions used it to make $108.5 million in electioneering communications. Supp. Brief for Appellee 22–23; FEC, Electioneering Communication Summary, online at http://fec.gov/finance/disclosure/ECSummary.shtml (all Internet materials as visited Jan. 18, 2010, and available in Clerk of Court's case file).

[28] Concededly, *Austin* and *McConnell* were constitutional decisions, and we have often said that "claims of *stare decisis* are at the weakest in that field, where our mistakes cannot be corrected by Congress." *Vieth* v. *Jubelirer,* 541 U. S. 267, 305 (2004) (plurality opinion). As a general matter, this principle is a sound one. But the principle only takes on real force when an earlier ruling has obstructed the normal democratic process; it is the fear of making "mistakes [that] cannot be corrected by Congress," *ibid.,* that motivates us to review constitutional precedents with a more critical eye. *Austin* and *McConnell* did not obstruct state or congressional legislative power in any way. Although it is unclear how high a bar today's decision will pose to future attempts to regulate corporate electioneering, it will clearly restrain much legislative action.

nell comes down to nothing more than its disagreement with their results. Virtually every one of its arguments was made and rejected in those cases, and the majority opinion is essentially an amalgamation of resuscitated dissents. The only relevant thing that has changed since *Austin* and *McConnell* is the composition of this Court. Today's ruling thus strikes at the vitals of *stare decisis*, "the means by which we ensure that the law will not merely change erratically, but will develop in a principled and intelligible fashion" that "permits society to presume that bedrock principles are founded in the law rather than in the proclivities of individuals." *Vasquez* v. *Hillery*, 474 U. S. 254, 265 (1986).

III

The novelty of the Court's procedural dereliction and its approach to *stare decisis* is matched by the novelty of its ruling on the merits. The ruling rests on several premises. First, the Court claims that *Austin* and *McConnell* have "banned" corporate speech. Second, it claims that the First Amendment precludes regulatory distinctions based on speaker identity, including the speaker's identity as a corporation. Third, it claims that *Austin* and *McConnell* were radical outliers in our First Amendment tradition and our campaign finance jurisprudence. Each of these claims is wrong.

The So-Called "Ban"

Pervading the Court's analysis is the ominous image of a "categorical ba[n]" on corporate speech. *Ante,* at 45. Indeed, the majority invokes the specter of a "ban" on nearly every page of its opinion. *Ante,* at 1, 4, 7, 10, 11, 12, 13, 16, 20, 21, 22, 23, 26, 27, 28, 29, 30, 31, 33, 35, 38, 40, 42, 45, 46, 47, 49, 54, 56. This characterization is highly misleading, and needs to be corrected.

In fact it already has been. Our cases have repeatedly

pointed out that, "[c]ontrary to the [majority's] critical assumptions," the statutes upheld in *Austin* and *McConnell* do "not impose an *absolute* ban on all forms of corporate political spending." *Austin*, 494 U. S., at 660; see also *McConnell*, 540 U. S., at 203–204; *Beaumont*, 539 U. S., at 162–163. For starters, both statutes provide exemptions for PACs, separate segregated funds established by a corporation for political purposes. See 2 U. S. C. §441b(b)(2)(C); Mich. Comp. Laws Ann. §169.255 (West 2005). "The ability to form and administer separate segregated funds," we observed in *McConnell*, "has provided corporations and unions with a constitutionally sufficient opportunity to engage in express advocacy. That has been this Court's unanimous view." 540 U. S., at 203.

Under BCRA, any corporation's "stockholders and their families and its executive or administrative personnel and their families" can pool their resources to finance electioneering communications. 2 U. S. C. §441b(b)(4)(A)(i). A significant and growing number of corporations avail themselves of this option;[29] during the most recent election cycle, corporate and union PACs raised nearly a billion dollars.[30] Administering a PAC entails some administrative burden, but so does complying with the disclaimer, disclosure, and reporting requirements that the Court today upholds, see *ante*, at 51, and no one has suggested that the burden is severe for a sophisticated for-profit corporation. To the extent the majority is worried about

---

[29] See FEC, Number of Federal PAC's Increases, http://fec.gov/press/ press2008/20080812paccount.shtml.

[30] See Supp. Brief for Appellee 16 (citing FEC statistics placing this figure at $840 million). The majority finds the PAC option inadequate in part because "[a] PAC is a separate association from the corporation." *Ante*, at 21. The formal "separateness" of PACs from their host corporations—which administer and control the PACs but which cannot funnel general treasury funds into them or force members to support them—is, of course, the whole point of the PAC mechanism.

this issue, it is important to keep in mind that we have no record to show how substantial the burden really is, just the majority's own unsupported factfinding, see *ante*, at 21–22. Like all other natural persons, every shareholder of every corporation remains entirely free under *Austin* and *McConnell* to do however much electioneering she pleases outside of the corporate form. The owners of a "mom & pop" store can simply place ads in their own names, rather than the store's. If ideologically aligned individuals wish to make unlimited expenditures through the corporate form, they may utilize an *MCFL* organization that has policies in place to avoid becoming a conduit for business or union interests. See *MCFL*, 479 U. S., at 263–264.

The laws upheld in *Austin* and *McConnell* leave open many additional avenues for corporations' political speech. Consider the statutory provision we are ostensibly evaluating in this case, BCRA §203. It has no application to genuine issue advertising—a category of corporate speech Congress found to be far more substantial than election-related advertising, see *McConnell*, 540 U. S., at 207—or to Internet, telephone, and print advocacy.[31] Like numer-

---

[31] Roaming far afield from the case at hand, the majority worries that the Government will use §203 to ban books, pamphlets, and blogs. *Ante*, at 20, 33, 49. Yet by its plain terms, §203 does not apply to printed material. See 2 U. S. C. §434(f)(3)(A)(i); see also 11 CFR §100.29(c)(1) ("[E]lectioneering communication does not include communications appearing in print media"). And in light of the ordinary understanding of the terms "broadcast, cable, [and] satellite," §434(f)(3)(A)(i), coupled with Congress' clear aim of targeting "a virtual torrent of televised election-related ads," *McConnell*, 540 U. S., at 207, we highly doubt that §203 could be interpreted to apply to a Web site or book that happens to be transmitted at some stage over airwaves or cable lines, or that the FEC would ever try to do so. See 11 CFR §100.26 (exempting most Internet communications from regulation as advertising); §100.155 (exempting uncompensated Internet activity from regulation as an expenditure); Supp. Brief for Center for Independent Media et al. as *Amici Curiae* 14 (explaining that "the FEC has

ous statutes, it exempts media companies' news stories, commentaries, and editorials from its electioneering restrictions, in recognition of the unique role played by the institutional press in sustaining public debate.[32]   See 2 U. S. C. §434(f)(3)(B)(i); *McConnell,* 540 U. S., at 208–209; see also *Austin,* 494 U. S., at 666–668.   It also allows corporations to spend unlimited sums on political communications with their executives and shareholders, §441b(b)(2)(A); 11 CFR §114.3(a)(1), to fund additional PAC activity through trade associations, 2 U. S. C. §441b(b)(4)(D), to distribute voting guides and voting records, 11 CFR §§114.4(c)(4)–(5), to underwrite voter registration and voter turnout activities, §114.3(c)(4); §114.4(c)(2), to host fundraising events for candidates within certain limits, §114.4(c); §114.2(f)(2), and to publicly endorse candidates through a press release and press conference, §114.4(c)(6).

At the time Citizens United brought this lawsuit, the only types of speech that could be regulated under §203 were: (1) broadcast, cable, or satellite communications;[33] (2) capable of reaching at least 50,000 persons in the relevant electorate;[34] (3) made within 30 days of a primary or 60 days of a general federal election;[35] (4) by a labor union or a non-*MCFL,* nonmedia corporation;[36] (5) paid for

---

consistently construed [BCRA's] media exemption to apply to a variety of non-traditional media"). If it should, the Government acknowledges "there would be quite [a] good as-applied challenge." Tr. of Oral Arg. 65 (Sept. 9, 2009).

[32] As the Government points out, with a media corporation there is also a lesser risk that investors will not understand, learn about, or support the advocacy messages that the corporation disseminates. Supp. Reply Brief for Appellee 10. Everyone knows and expects that media outlets may seek to influence elections in this way.

[33] 2 U. S. C. §434(f)(3)(A)(i).

[34] §434(f)(3)(C).

[35] §434(f)(3)(A)(i)(II).

[36] §441b(b); *McConnell,* 540 U. S., at 211.

with general treasury funds;[37] and (6) "susceptible of no
reasonable interpretation other than as an appeal to vote
for or against a specific candidate."[38] The category of
communications meeting all of these criteria is not trivial,
but the notion that corporate political speech has been
"suppress[ed] . . . altogether," *ante*, at 2, that corporations
have been "exclu[ded] . . . from the general public dialogue," *ante*, at 25, or that a work of fiction such as *Mr.
Smith Goes to Washington* might be covered, *ante*, at 56–
57, is nonsense.[39] Even the plaintiffs in *McConnell*, who
had every incentive to depict BCRA as negatively as possible, declined to argue that §203's prohibition on certain
uses of general treasury funds amounts to a complete ban.
See 540 U. S., at 204.

In many ways, then, §203 functions as a source restriction or a time, place, and manner restriction. It applies in
a viewpoint-neutral fashion to a narrow subset of advocacy
messages about clearly identified candidates for federal
office, made during discrete time periods through discrete
channels. In the case at hand, all Citizens United needed
to do to broadcast *Hillary* right before the primary was to
abjure business contributions or use the funds in its PAC,
which by its own account is "one of the most active conservative PACs in America," Citizens United Political Victory

---

[37] §441b(b)(2)(C).

[38] *WRTL*, 551 U. S. 449, 470 (2007) (opinion of ROBERTS, C. J.).

[39] It is likewise nonsense to suggest that the FEC's "'business is to
censor.'" *Ante*, at 18 (quoting *Freedman* v. *Maryland*, 380 U. S. 51, 57
(1965)). The FEC's business is to administer and enforce the campaign
finance laws. The regulatory body at issue in *Freedman* was a state
Board of Censors that had virtually unfettered discretion to bar distribution of motion picture films it deemed not to be "moral and proper."
See *id.*, at 52–53, and n. 2. No movie could be shown in the State of
Maryland that was not first approved and licensed by the Board of
Censors. *Id.*, at 52, n. 1. It is an understatement to say that *Freedman*
is not on point, and the majority's characterization of the FEC is deeply
disconcerting.

Fund, http://www.cupvf.org/.[40]

So let us be clear: Neither *Austin* nor *McConnell* held or implied that corporations may be silenced; the FEC is not a "censor"; and in the years since these cases were decided, corporations have continued to play a major role in the national dialogue. Laws such as §203 target a class of communications that is especially likely to corrupt the political process, that is at least one degree removed from the views of individual citizens, and that may not even reflect the views of those who pay for it. Such laws burden political speech, and that is always a serious matter, demanding careful scrutiny. But the majority's incessant talk of a "ban" aims at a straw man.

Identity-Based Distinctions

The second pillar of the Court's opinion is its assertion that "the Government cannot restrict political speech based on the speaker's . . . identity." *Ante*, at 30; accord, *ante,* at 1, 24, 26, 30, 31, 32, 33, 34, 49, 50. The case on which it relies for this proposition is *First Nat. Bank of Boston* v. *Bellotti*, 435 U. S. 765 (1978). As I shall explain, *infra*, at 52–55, the holding in that case was far narrower than the Court implies. Like its paeans to unfettered discourse, the Court's denunciation of identity-based distinctions may have rhetorical appeal but it obscures reality.

"Our jurisprudence over the past 216 years has rejected an absolutist interpretation" of the First Amendment. *WRTL*, 551 U. S., at 482 (opinion of ROBERTS, C. J.). The

---

[40] Citizens United has administered this PAC for over a decade. See Defendant FEC's Memorandum in Opposition to Plaintiff's Second Motion for Preliminary Injunction in No. 07–2240 (ARR, RCL, RWR) (DC), p. 20. Citizens United also operates multiple "527" organizations that engage in partisan political activity. See Defendant FEC's Statement of Material Facts as to Which There Is No Genuine Dispute in No. 07–2240 (DC), ¶¶ 22–24.

Opinion of STEVENS, J.

First Amendment provides that "Congress shall make no
law . . . abridging the freedom of speech, or of the press."
Apart perhaps from measures designed to protect the
press, that text might seem to permit no distinctions of
any kind. Yet in a variety of contexts, we have held that
speech can be regulated differentially on account of the
speaker's identity, when identity is understood in categorical or institutional terms. The Government routinely
places special restrictions on the speech rights of students,[41] prisoners,[42] members of the Armed Forces,[43] foreigners,[44] and its own employees.[45] When such restrictions are justified by a legitimate governmental interest,
they do not necessarily raise constitutional problems.[46] In

---

[41] See, e.g., Bethel School Dist. No. 403 v. Fraser, 478 U. S. 675, 682
(1986) ("[T]he constitutional rights of students in public school are not
automatically coextensive with the rights of adults in other settings").

[42] See, e.g., Jones v. North Carolina Prisoners' Labor Union, Inc., 433
U. S. 119, 129 (1977) ("In a prison context, an inmate does not retain
those First Amendment rights that are inconsistent with his status as a
prisoner or with the legitimate penological objectives of the corrections
system" (internal quotation marks omitted)).

[43] See, e.g., Parker v. Levy, 417 U. S. 733, 758 (1974) ("While the
members of the military are not excluded from the protection granted
by the First Amendment, the different character of the military community and of the military mission requires a different application of
those protections").

[44] See, e.g., 2 U. S. C. §441e(a)(1) (foreign nationals may not directly
or indirectly make contributions or independent expenditures in connection with a U. S. election).

[45] See, e.g., Civil Service Comm'n v. Letter Carriers, 413 U. S. 548
(1973) (upholding statute prohibiting Executive Branch employees from
taking "any active part in political management or in political campaigns" (internal quotation marks omitted)); Public Workers v. Mitchell,
330 U. S. 75 (1947) (same); United States v. Wurzbach, 280 U. S. 396
(1930) (upholding statute prohibiting federal employees from making
contributions to Members of Congress for "any political purpose whatever" (internal quotation marks omitted)); Ex parte Curtis, 106 U. S.
371 (1882) (upholding statute prohibiting certain federal employees
from giving money to other employees for political purposes).

[46] The majority states that the cases just cited are "inapposite" be-

contrast to the blanket rule that the majority espouses, our cases recognize that the Government's interests may be more or less compelling with respect to different classes of speakers,[47] cf. *Minneapolis Star & Tribune Co.* v. *Minnesota Comm'r of Revenue,* 460 U. S. 575, 585 (1983) ("[D]ifferential treatment" is constitutionally suspect "*unless* justified by some special characteristic" of the regulated class of speakers (emphasis added)), and that the constitutional rights of certain categories of speakers, in certain contexts, "'are not automatically coextensive with the rights'" that are normally accorded to members of our society, *Morse* v. *Frederick,* 551 U. S. 393, 396–397, 404 (2007) (quoting *Bethel School Dist. No. 403* v. *Fraser,* 478 U. S. 675, 682 (1986)).

The free speech guarantee thus does not render every other public interest an illegitimate basis for qualifying a speaker's autonomy; society could scarcely function if it did. It is fair to say that our First Amendment doctrine has "frowned on" certain identity-based distinctions, *Los Angeles Police Dept.* v. *United Reporting Publishing Corp.,*

---

cause they "stand only for the proposition that there are certain governmental functions that cannot operate without some restrictions on particular kinds of speech." *Ante,* at 25. The majority's creative suggestion that these cases stand only for that one proposition is quite implausible. In any event, the proposition lies at the heart of this case, as Congress and half the state legislatures have concluded, over many decades, that their core functions of administering elections and passing legislation cannot operate effectively without some narrow restrictions on corporate electioneering paid for by general treasury funds.

[47] Outside of the law, of course, it is a commonplace that the identity and incentives of the speaker might be relevant to an assessment of his speech. See Aristotle, Poetics 43–44 (M. Heath transl. 1996) ("In evaluating any utterance or action, one must take into account not just the moral qualities of what is actually done or said, but also the identity of the agent or speaker, the addressee, the occasion, the means, and the motive"). The insight that the identity of speakers is a proper subject of regulatory concern, it bears noting, motivates the disclaimer and disclosure provisions that the Court today upholds.

528 U. S. 32, 47, n. 4 (1999) (STEVENS, J., dissenting), particularly those that may reflect invidious discrimination or preferential treatment of a politically powerful group. But it is simply incorrect to suggest that we have prohibited all legislative distinctions based on identity or content. Not even close.

The election context is distinctive in many ways, and the Court, of course, is right that the First Amendment closely guards political speech. But in this context, too, the authority of legislatures to enact viewpoint-neutral regulations based on content and identity is well settled. We have, for example, allowed state-run broadcasters to exclude independent candidates from televised debates. *Arkansas Ed. Television Comm'n v. Forbes*, 523 U. S. 666 (1998).[48] We have upheld statutes that prohibit the distribution or display of campaign materials near a polling place. *Burson v. Freeman*, 504 U. S. 191 (1992).[49] Although we have not reviewed them directly, we have never cast doubt on laws that place special restrictions on campaign spending by foreign nationals. See, *e.g.*, 2 U. S. C. §441e(a)(1). And we have consistently approved laws that bar Government employees, but not others, from contrib-

---

[48] I dissented in *Forbes* because the broadcaster's decision to exclude the respondent from its debate was done "on the basis of entirely subjective, ad hoc judgments," 523 U. S., at 690, that suggested anticompetitive viewpoint discrimination, *id.*, at 693–694, and lacked a compelling justification. Needless to say, my concerns do not apply to the instant case.

[49] The law at issue in *Burson* was far from unusual. "[A]ll 50 States," the Court observed, "limit access to the areas in or around polling places." 504 U. S., at 206; see also Note, 91 Ky. L. J. 715, 729, n. 89, 747–769 (2003) (collecting statutes). I dissented in *Burson* because the evidence adduced to justify Tennessee's law was "exceptionally thin," 504 U. S., at 219, and "the reason for [the] restriction [had] disappear[ed]" over time, *id.*, at 223. "In short," I concluded, "Tennessee ha[d] failed to point to any legitimate interest that would justify its selective regulation of campaign-related expression." *Id.*, at 225. These criticisms are inapplicable to the case before us.

uting to or participating in political activities. See n. 45, *supra.* These statutes burden the political expression of one class of speakers, namely, civil servants. Yet we have sustained them on the basis of longstanding practice and Congress' reasoned judgment that certain regulations which leave "untouched full participation . . . in political decisions at the ballot box," *Civil Service Comm'n* v. *Letter Carriers,* 413 U. S. 548, 556 (1973) (internal quotation marks omitted), help ensure that public officials are "sufficiently free from improper influences," *id.,* at 564, and that "confidence in the system of representative Government is not . . . eroded to a disastrous extent," *id.,* at 565.

The same logic applies to this case with additional force because it is the identity of corporations, rather than individuals, that the Legislature has taken into account. As we have unanimously observed, legislatures are entitled to decide "that the special characteristics of the corporate structure require particularly careful regulation" in an electoral context. *NRWC,* 459 U. S., at 209–210.[50] Not only has the distinctive potential of corporations to corrupt the electoral process long been recognized, but within the area of campaign finance, corporate spending is also "furthest from the core of political expression, since corporations' First Amendment speech and association interests are derived largely from those of their members and of the public in receiving information," *Beaumont,* 539 U. S., at 161, n. 8 (citation omitted). Campaign finance distinctions based on corporate identity tend to be less worrisome, in other words, because the "speakers" are not natural persons, much less members of our political community, and

---

[50] They are likewise entitled to regulate media corporations differently from other corporations "to ensure that the law 'does not hinder or prevent the institutional press from reporting on, and publishing editorials about, newsworthy events.'" *McConnell,* 540 U. S., at 208 (quoting *Austin* v. *Michigan Chamber of Commerce,* 494 U. S. 652, 668 (1990)).

the governmental interests are of the highest order. Furthermore, when corporations, as a class, are distinguished from noncorporations, as a class, there is a lesser risk that regulatory distinctions will reflect invidious discrimination or political favoritism.

If taken seriously, our colleagues' assumption that the identity of a speaker has *no* relevance to the Government's ability to regulate political speech would lead to some remarkable conclusions. Such an assumption would have accorded the propaganda broadcasts to our troops by "Tokyo Rose" during World War II the same protection as speech by Allied commanders. More pertinently, it would appear to afford the same protection to multinational corporations controlled by foreigners as to individual Americans: To do otherwise, after all, could "'enhance the relative voice'" of some (*i.e.*, humans) over others (*i.e.*, nonhumans). *Ante*, at 33 (quoting *Buckley*, 424 U. S., at 49).[51] Under the majority's view, I suppose it may be a First Amendment problem that corporations are not permitted to vote, given that voting is, among other things, a

---

[51] The Court all but confesses that a categorical approach to speaker identity is untenable when it acknowledges that Congress might be allowed to take measures aimed at "preventing foreign individuals or associations from influencing our Nation's political process." *Ante*, at 46–47. Such measures have been a part of U. S. campaign finance law for many years. The notion that Congress might lack the authority to distinguish foreigners from citizens in the regulation of electioneering would certainly have surprised the Framers, whose "obsession with foreign influence derived from a fear that foreign powers and individuals had no basic investment in the well-being of the country." Teachout, The Anti-Corruption Principle, 94 Cornell L. Rev. 341, 393, n. 245 (2009) (hereinafter Teachout); see also U. S. Const., Art. I, §9, cl. 8 ("[N]o Person holding any Office of Profit or Trust . . . shall, without the Consent of the Congress, accept of any present, Emolument, Office, or Title, of any kind whatever, from any King, Prince, or foreign State"). Professor Teachout observes that a corporation might be analogized to a foreign power in this respect, "inasmuch as its legal loyalties necessarily exclude patriotism." Teachout 393, n. 245.

form of speech.[52]

In short, the Court dramatically overstates its critique of identity-based distinctions, without ever explaining why corporate identity demands the same treatment as individual identity. Only the most wooden approach to the First Amendment could justify the unprecedented line it seeks to draw.

Our First Amendment Tradition

A third fulcrum of the Court's opinion is the idea that *Austin* and *McConnell* are radical outliers, "aberration[s]," in our First Amendment tradition. *Ante,* at 39; see also *ante,* at 45, 56 (professing fidelity to "our law and our tradition"). The Court has it exactly backwards. It is today's holding that is the radical departure from what had been settled First Amendment law. To see why, it is useful to take a long view.

1. *Original Understandings*

Let us start from the beginning. The Court invokes "ancient First Amendment principles," *ante,* at 1 (internal quotation marks omitted), and original understandings, *ante,* at 37–38, to defend today's ruling, yet it makes only a perfunctory attempt to ground its analysis in the principles or understandings of those who drafted and ratified the Amendment. Perhaps this is because there is not a scintilla of evidence to support the notion that anyone

---

[52] See A. Bickel, The Supreme Court and the Idea of Progress 59–60 (1978); A. Meiklejohn, Political Freedom: The Constitutional Powers of the People 39–40 (1965); Tokaji, First Amendment Equal Protection: On Discretion, Inequality, and Participation, 101 Mich. L. Rev. 2409, 2508–2509 (2003). Of course, voting is not speech in a pure or formal sense, but then again neither is a campaign expenditure; both are nevertheless communicative acts aimed at influencing electoral outcomes. Cf. Strauss, Corruption, Equality, and Campaign Finance Reform, 94 Colum. L. Rev. 1369, 1383–1384 (1994) (hereinafter Strauss).

believed it would preclude regulatory distinctions based on the corporate form. To the extent that the Framers' views are discernible and relevant to the disposition of this case, they would appear to cut strongly against the majority's position.

This is not only because the Framers and their contemporaries conceived of speech more narrowly than we now think of it, see Bork, Neutral Principles and Some First Amendment Problems, 47 Ind. L. J. 1, 22 (1971), but also because they held very different views about the nature of the First Amendment right and the role of corporations in society. Those few corporations that existed at the founding were authorized by grant of a special legislative charter.[53] Corporate sponsors would petition the legislature, and the legislature, if amenable, would issue a charter that specified the corporation's powers and purposes and "authoritatively fixed the scope and content of corporate organization," including "the internal structure of the

---

[53] Scholars have found that only a handful of business corporations were issued charters during the colonial period, and only a few hundred during all of the 18th century. See E. Dodd, American Business Corporations Until 1860, p. 197 (1954); L. Friedman, A History of American Law 188–189 (2d ed. 1985); Baldwin, American Business Corporations Before 1789, 8 Am. Hist. Rev. 449, 450–459 (1903). JUSTICE SCALIA quibbles with these figures; whereas we say that "a few hundred" charters were issued to business corporations during the 18th century, he says that the number is "approximately 335." Ante, at 2 (concurring opinion). JUSTICE SCALIA also raises the more serious point that it is improper to assess these figures by today's standards, ante, at 3, though I believe he fails to substantiate his claim that "the corporation was a familiar figure in American economic life" by the century's end, ibid. (internal quotation marks omitted). His formulation of that claim is also misleading, because the relevant reference point is not 1800 but the date of the First Amendment's ratification, in 1791. And at that time, the number of business charters must have been significantly smaller than 335, because the pace of chartering only began to pick up steam in the last decade of the 18th century. More than half of the century's total business charters were issued between 1796 and 1800. Friedman, History of American Law, at 189.

corporation." J. Hurst, The Legitimacy of the Business Corporation in the Law of the United States 1780–1970, pp. 15–16 (1970) (reprint 2004). Corporations were created, supervised, and conceptualized as quasi-public entities, "designed to serve a social function for the state." Handlin & Handlin, Origin of the American Business Corporation, 5 J. Econ. Hist. 1, 22 (1945). It was "assumed that [they] were legally privileged organizations that had to be closely scrutinized by the legislature because their purposes had to be made consistent with public welfare." R. Seavoy, Origins of the American Business Corporation, 1784–1855, p. 5 (1982).

The individualized charter mode of incorporation reflected the "cloud of disfavor under which corporations labored" in the early years of this Nation. 1 W. Fletcher, Cyclopedia of the Law of Corporations §2, p. 8 (rev. ed. 2006); see also *Louis K. Liggett Co.* v. *Lee*, 288 U. S. 517, 548–549 (1933) (Brandeis, J., dissenting) (discussing fears of the "evils" of business corporations); L. Friedman, A History of American Law 194 (2d ed. 1985) ("The word 'soulless' constantly recurs in debates over corporations. . . . Corporations, it was feared, could concentrate the worst urges of whole groups of men"). Thomas Jefferson famously fretted that corporations would subvert the Republic.[54] General incorporation statutes, and widespread acceptance of business corporations as socially useful actors, did not emerge until the 1800's. See Hansmann & Kraakman, The End of History for Corporate Law, 89 Geo. L. J. 439, 440 (2001) (hereinafter Hansmann & Kraakman) ("[A]ll general business corporation statutes appear to date from well after 1800").

------

[54] See Letter from Thomas Jefferson to Tom Logan (Nov. 12, 1816), in 12 The Works of Thomas Jefferson 42, 44 (P. Ford ed. 1905) ("I hope we shall . . . crush in [its] birth the aristocracy of our monied corporations which dare already to challenge our government to a trial of strength and bid defiance to the laws of our country").

The Framers thus took it as a given that corporations could be comprehensively regulated in the service of the public welfare.   Unlike our colleagues, they had little trouble distinguishing corporations from human beings, and when they constitutionalized the right to free speech in the First Amendment, it was the free speech of individual Americans that they had in mind.[55] While individuals might join together to exercise their speech rights, business corporations, at least, were plainly not seen as facilitating such associational or expressive ends.   Even "the notion that business corporations could invoke the First Amendment would probably have been quite a novelty," given that "at the time, the legitimacy of every corporate activity was thought to rest entirely in a concession of the sovereign."   Shelledy, Autonomy, Debate, and Corporate Speech, 18 Hastings Const. L. Q. 541, 578 (1991); cf. *Trustees of Dartmouth College* v. *Woodward*, 4 Wheat. 518, 636

---

[55] In normal usage then, as now, the term "speech" referred to oral communications by individuals. See, *e.g.*, 2 S. Johnson, Dictionary of the English Language 1853–1854 (4th ed. 1773) (reprinted 1978) (listing as primary definition of "speech": "The power of articulate utterance; the power of expressing thoughts by vocal words"); 2 N. Webster, American Dictionary of the English Language (1828) (reprinted 1970) (listing as primary definition of "speech": "The faculty of uttering articulate sounds or words, as in human beings; the faculty of expressing thoughts by words or articulate sounds. *Speech* was given to man by his Creator for the noblest purposes"). Indeed, it has been "claimed that the notion of institutional speech . . . did not exist in post-revolutionary America." Fagundes, State Actors as First Amendment Speakers, 100 Nw. U. L. Rev. 1637, 1654 (2006); see also Bezanson, Institutional Speech, 80 Iowa L. Rev. 735, 775 (1995) ("In the intellectual heritage of the eighteenth century, the idea that free speech was individual and personal was deeply rooted and clearly manifest in the writings of Locke, Milton, and others on whom the framers of the Constitution and the Bill of Rights drew"). Given that corporations were conceived of as artificial entities and do not have the technical capacity to "speak," the burden of establishing that the Framers and ratifiers understood "the freedom of speech" to encompass corporate speech is, I believe, far heavier than the majority acknowledges.

(1819) (Marshall, C. J.) ("A corporation is an artificial being, invisible, intangible, and existing only in contemplation of law. Being the mere creature of law, it possesses only those properties which the charter of its creation confers upon it"); Eule, Promoting Speaker Diversity: Austin and Metro Broadcasting, 1990 S. Ct. Rev. 105, 129 ("The framers of the First Amendment could scarcely have anticipated its application to the corporation form. That, of course, ought not to be dispositive. What is compelling, however, is an understanding of who was supposed to be the beneficiary of the free speech guaranty—the individual"). In light of these background practices and understandings, it seems to me implausible that the Framers believed "the freedom of speech" would extend equally to all corporate speakers, much less that it would preclude legislatures from taking limited measures to guard against corporate capture of elections.

The Court observes that the Framers drew on diverse intellectual sources, communicated through newspapers, and aimed to provide greater freedom of speech than had existed in England. *Ante,* at 37. From these (accurate) observations, the Court concludes that "[t]he First Amendment was certainly not understood to condone the suppression of political speech in society's most salient media." *Ibid.* This conclusion is far from certain, given that many historians believe the Framers were focused on prior restraints on publication and did not understand the First Amendment to "prevent the subsequent punishment of such [publications] as may be deemed contrary to the public welfare." *Near* v. *Minnesota ex rel. Olson,* 283 U. S. 697, 714 (1931). Yet, even if the majority's conclusion were correct, it would tell us only that the First Amendment was understood to protect political speech *in* certain media. It would tell us little about whether the Amendment was understood to protect general treasury electioneering expenditures *by* corporations, *and to what extent.*

As a matter of original expectations, then, it seems absurd to think that the First Amendment prohibits legislatures from taking into account the corporate identity of a sponsor of electoral advocacy. As a matter of original meaning, it likewise seems baseless—unless one evaluates the First Amendment's "principles," *ante,* at 1, 48, or its "purpose," *ante,* at 5 (opinion of ROBERTS, C. J.), at such a high level of generality that the historical understandings of the Amendment cease to be a meaningful constraint on the judicial task. This case sheds a revelatory light on the assumption of some that an impartial judge's application of an originalist methodology is likely to yield more determinate answers, or to play a more decisive role in the decisional process, than his or her views about sound policy.

JUSTICE SCALIA criticizes the foregoing discussion for failing to adduce statements from the founding era showing that corporations were understood to be excluded from the First Amendment's free speech guarantee. *Ante,* at 1–2, 9. Of course, JUSTICE SCALIA adduces no statements to suggest the contrary proposition, or even to suggest that the contrary proposition better reflects the kind of right that the drafters and ratifiers of the Free Speech Clause thought they were enshrining. Although JUSTICE SCALIA makes a perfectly sensible argument that an individual's right to speak entails a right to speak with others for a common cause, cf. *MCFL,* 479 U. S. 238, he does not explain why those two rights must be precisely identical, or why that principle applies to electioneering by corporations that serve no "common cause." *Ante,* at 8. Nothing in his account dislodges my basic point that members of the founding generation held a cautious view of corporate power and a narrow view of corporate rights (not that they "despised" corporations, *ante,* at 2), and that they conceptualized speech in individualistic terms. If no prominent Framer bothered to articulate that corporate speech would have lesser status than individual speech, that may well be because the contrary proposition—if not also the very notion of "corporate speech"—was inconceivable.[56]

JUSTICE SCALIA also emphasizes the unqualified nature of the First Amendment text. *Ante,* at 2, 8. Yet he would seemingly read out the Free Press Clause: How else could he claim that my purported views on newspapers must track my views on corporations generally? *Ante,* at 6.[57] Like virtually all modern lawyers, JUSTICE SCALIA presumably believes that the First Amendment restricts the Executive, even though its language refers to Congress alone. In any event, the text only leads us back to the questions who or what is guaranteed "the freedom of speech," and, just as critically, what that freedom consists of and under what circumstances it may be limited. JUSTICE SCALIA appears to believe that because corporations are created and utilized by individuals, it follows (as

---

[56] Postratification practice bolsters the conclusion that the First Amendment, "as originally understood," *ante,* at 37, did not give corporations political speech rights on a par with the rights of individuals. Well into the modern era of general incorporation statutes, "[t]he common law was generally interpreted as prohibiting corporate political participation," *First Nat. Bank of Boston* v. *Bellotti,* 435 U. S. 765, 819 (1978) (White, J., dissenting), and this Court did not recognize *any* First Amendment protections for corporations until the middle part of the 20th century, see *ante,* at 25–26 (listing cases).

[57] In fact, the Free Press Clause might be turned against JUSTICE SCALIA, for two reasons. First, we learn from it that the drafters of the First Amendment did draw distinctions—explicit distinctions—between types of "speakers," or speech outlets or forms. Second, the Court's strongest historical evidence all relates to the Framers' views on the press, see *ante,* at 37–38; *ante,* at 4–6 (SCALIA, J., concurring), yet while the Court tries to sweep this evidence into the Free Speech Clause, the Free Press Clause provides a more natural textual home. The text and history highlighted by our colleagues suggests why one type of corporation, those that are part of the press, might be able to claim special First Amendment status, and therefore why some kinds of "identity"-based distinctions might be permissible after all. Once one accepts that much, the intellectual edifice of the majority opinion crumbles.

night the day) that their electioneering must be equally protected by the First Amendment and equally immunized from expenditure limits. See *ante*, at 7–8. That conclusion certainly does not follow as a logical matter, and JUSTICE SCALIA fails to explain why the original public meaning leads it to follow as a matter of interpretation.

The truth is we cannot be certain how a law such as BCRA §203 meshes with the original meaning of the First Amendment.[58] I have given several reasons why I believe the Constitution would have been understood then, and ought to be understood now, to permit reasonable restrictions on corporate electioneering, and I will give many more reasons in the pages to come. The Court enlists the Framers in its defense without seriously grappling with their understandings of corporations or the free speech right, or with the republican principles that underlay those understandings.

In fairness, our campaign finance jurisprudence has never attended very closely to the views of the Framers, see *Randall* v. *Sorrell*, 548 U. S. 230, 280 (2006) (STEVENS, J., dissenting), whose political universe differed profoundly from that of today. We have long since held that corporations are covered by the First Amendment, and many legal scholars have long since rejected the concession theory of the corporation. But "historical context is usually relevant," *ibid.* (internal quotation marks omitted), and in light of the Court's effort to cast itself as guardian of ancient values, it pays to remember that nothing in our constitutional history dictates today's outcome. To the contrary, this history helps illuminate just how extraordinarily dissonant the decision is.

---

[58] Cf. L. Levy, Legacy of Suppression: Freedom of Speech and Press in Early American History 4 (1960) ("The meaning of no other clause of the Bill of Rights at the time of its framing and ratification has been so obscure to us" as the Free Speech and Press Clause).

2. *Legislative and Judicial Interpretation*

A century of more recent history puts to rest any notion that today's ruling is faithful to our First Amendment tradition. At the federal level, the express distinction between corporate and individual political spending on elections stretches back to 1907, when Congress passed the Tillman Act, ch. 420, 34 Stat. 864, banning all corporate contributions to candidates. The Senate Report on the legislation observed that "[t]he evils of the use of [corporate] money in connection with political elections are so generally recognized that the committee deems it unnecessary to make any argument in favor of the general purpose of this measure. It is in the interest of good government and calculated to promote purity in the selection of public officials." S. Rep. No. 3056, 59th Cong., 1st Sess., 2 (1906). President Roosevelt, in his 1905 annual message to Congress, declared:

> "'All contributions by corporations to any political committee or for any political purpose should be forbidden by law; directors should not be permitted to use stockholders' money for such purposes; and, moreover, a prohibition of this kind would be, as far as it went, an effective method of stopping the evils aimed at in corrupt practices acts.'" *United States* v. *Automobile Workers,* 352 U. S. 567, 572 (1957) (quoting 40 Cong. Rec. 96).

The Court has surveyed the history leading up to the Tillman Act several times, see *WRTL,* 551 U. S., at 508–510 (Souter, J., dissenting); *McConnell,* 540 U. S., at 115; *Automobile Workers,* 352 U. S., at 570–575, and I will refrain from doing so again. It is enough to say that the Act was primarily driven by two pressing concerns: first, the enormous power corporations had come to wield in federal elections, with the accompanying threat of both actual corruption and a public perception of corruption;

and second, a respect for the interest of shareholders and members in preventing the use of their money to support candidates they opposed. See *ibid.; United States* v. *CIO,* 335 U. S. 106, 113 (1948); Winkler, "Other People's Money": Corporations, Agency Costs, and Campaign Finance Law, 92 Geo. L. J. 871 (2004).

Over the years, the limitations on corporate political spending have been modified in a number of ways, as Congress responded to changes in the American economy and political practices that threatened to displace the commonweal. Justice Souter recently traced these developments at length.[59] *WRTL,* 551 U. S., at 507–519 (dissenting opinion); see also *McConnell,* 540 U. S., at 115–133; *McConnell,* 251 F. Supp. 2d, at 188–205. The Taft-Hartley Act of 1947 is of special significance for this case. In that Act passed more than 60 years ago, Congress extended the prohibition on corporate support of candidates to cover not only direct contributions, but independent expenditures as well. Labor Management Relations Act, 1947, §304, 61 Stat. 159. The bar on contributions "was being so narrowly construed" that corporations were easily able to defeat the purposes of the Act by supporting candidates through other means. *WRTL,* 551 U. S., at 511 (Souter, J., dissenting) (citing S. Rep. No. 1, 80th Cong., 1st Sess., 38–39 (1947)).

Our colleagues emphasize that in two cases from the middle of the 20th century, several Justices wrote sepa-

---

[59]As the majority notes, there is some academic debate about the precise origins of these developments. *Ante,* at 48; see also n. 19, *supra.* There is *always* some academic debate about such developments; the motives of legislatures are never entirely clear or unitary. Yet the basic shape and trajectory of 20th-century campaign finance reform are clear, and one need not take a naïve or triumphalist view of this history to find it highly relevant. The Court's skepticism does nothing to mitigate the absurdity of its claim that *Austin* and *McConnell* were outliers. Nor does it alter the fact that five Justices today destroy a longstanding American practice.

rately to criticize the expenditure restriction as applied to unions, even though the Court declined to pass on its constitutionality. *Ante*, at 27–28. Two features of these cases are of far greater relevance. First, those Justices were writing separately; which is to say, their position failed to command a majority. Prior to today, this was a fact we found significant in evaluating precedents. Second, each case in this line expressed support for the principle that corporate and union political speech financed with PAC funds, collected voluntarily from the organization's stockholders or members, receives greater protection than speech financed with general treasury funds.[60]

---

[60] See *Pipefitters* v. *United States*, 407 U. S. 385, 409, 414–415 (1972) (reading the statutory bar on corporate and union campaign spending not to apply to "the voluntary donations of employees," when maintained in a separate account, because "[t]he dominant [legislative] concern in requiring that contributions be voluntary was, after all, to protect the dissenting stockholder or union member"); *Automobile Workers*, 352 U. S., at 592 (advising the District Court to consider on remand whether the broadcast in question was "paid for out of the general dues of the union membership or [whether] the funds [could] be fairly said to have obtained on a voluntary basis"); *United States* v. *CIO*, 335 U. S. 106, 123 (1948) (observing that "funds voluntarily contributed [by union members or corporate stockholders] for election purposes" might not be covered by the expenditure bar). Both the *Pipefitters* and the *Automobile Workers* Court approvingly referenced Congress' goal of reducing "the effect of aggregated wealth on federal elections," understood as wealth drawn from a corporate or union general treasury without the stockholders' or members' "free and knowing choice." *Pipefitters*, 407 U. S., at 416; see *Automobile Workers*, 352 U. S., at 582.

The two dissenters in *Pipefitters* would not have read the statutory provision in question, a successor to §304 of the Taft-Hartley Act, to allow such robust use of corporate and union funds to finance otherwise prohibited electioneering. "This opening of the door to extensive corporate and union influence on the elective and legislative processes," Justice Powell wrote, "must be viewed with genuine concern. This seems to me to be a regressive step as contrasted with the numerous legislative and judicial actions in recent years designed to assure that elections are indeed free and representative." 407 U. S., at 450 (opinion

This principle was carried forward when Congress enacted comprehensive campaign finance reform in the Federal Election Campaign Act of 1971 (FECA), 86 Stat. 3, which retained the restriction on using general treasury funds for contributions and expenditures, 2 U. S. C. §441b(a). FECA codified the option for corporations and unions to create PACs to finance contributions and expenditures forbidden to the corporation or union itself. §441b(b).

By the time Congress passed FECA in 1971, the bar on corporate contributions and expenditures had become such an accepted part of federal campaign finance regulation that when a large number of plaintiffs, including several nonprofit corporations, challenged virtually every aspect of the Act in *Buckley,* 424 U. S. 1, no one even bothered to argue that the bar as such was unconstitutional. *Buckley* famously (or infamously) distinguished direct contributions from independent expenditures, *id.,* at 58–59, but its silence on corporations only reinforced the understanding that corporate expenditures could be treated differently from individual expenditures. "Since our decision in *Buckley,* Congress' power to prohibit corporations and unions from using funds in their treasuries to finance advertisements expressly advocating the election or defeat of candidates in federal elections has been firmly embedded in our law." *McConnell,* 540 U. S., at 203.

Thus, it was unremarkable, in a 1982 case holding that Congress could bar nonprofit corporations from soliciting nonmembers for PAC funds, that then-Justice Rehnquist wrote for a unanimous Court that Congress' "careful legislative adjustment of the federal electoral laws, in a cautious advance, step by step, to account for the particular legal and economic attributes of corporations . . . warrants considerable deference," and "reflects a permissible as-

---

of Powell, J., joined by Burger, C. J.).

sessment of the dangers posed by those entities to the electoral process." *NRWC*, 459 U. S., at 209 (internal quotation marks and citation omitted). "The governmental interest in preventing both actual corruption and the appearance of corruption of elected representatives has long been recognized," the unanimous Court observed, "and there is no reason why it may not . . . be accomplished by treating . . . corporations . . . differently from individuals." *Id.*, at 210–211.

The corporate/individual distinction was not questioned by the Court's disposition, in 1986, of a challenge to the expenditure restriction as applied to a distinctive type of nonprofit corporation. In *MCFL*, 479 U. S. 238, we stated again "that 'the special characteristics of the corporate structure require particularly careful regulation,'" *id.*, at 256 (quoting *NRWC*, 459 U. S., at 209–210), and again we acknowledged that the Government has a legitimate interest in "regulat[ing] the substantial aggregations of wealth amassed by the special advantages which go with the corporate form," 479 U. S., at 257 (internal quotation marks omitted). Those aggregations can distort the "free trade in ideas" crucial to candidate elections, *ibid.*, at the expense of members or shareholders who may disagree with the object of the expenditures, *id.*, at 260 (internal quotation marks omitted). What the Court held by a 5-to-4 vote was that a limited class of corporations must be allowed to use their general treasury funds for independent expenditures, because Congress' interests in protecting shareholders and "restrict[ing] 'the influence of political war chests funneled through the corporate form,'" *id.*, at 257 (quoting *FEC* v. *National Conservative Political Action Comm.*, 470 U. S. 480, 501 (1985) *(NCPAC)*), did not apply to corporations that were structurally insulated from those concerns.[61]

---

[61] Specifically, these corporations had to meet three conditions. First,

It is worth remembering for present purposes that the four *MCFL* dissenters, led by Chief Justice Rehnquist, thought the Court was carrying the First Amendment *too far*. They would have recognized congressional authority to bar general treasury electioneering expenditures even by this class of nonprofits; they acknowledged that "the threat from corporate political activity will vary depending on the particular characteristics of a given corporation," but believed these "distinctions among corporations" were "distinctions in degree," not "in kind," and thus "more properly drawn by the Legislature than by the Judiciary." 479 U. S., at 268 (opinion of Rehnquist, C. J.) (internal quotation marks omitted). Not a single Justice suggested that regulation of corporate political speech could be no more stringent than of speech by an individual.

Four years later, in *Austin*, 494 U. S. 652, we considered whether corporations falling outside the *MCFL* exception could be barred from using general treasury funds to make independent expenditures in support of, or in opposition to, candidates. We held they could be. Once again recognizing the importance of "the integrity of the marketplace of political ideas" in candidate elections, *MCFL*, 479 U. S., at 257, we noted that corporations have "special advantages—such as limited liability, perpetual life, and favorable treatment of the accumulation and distribution of assets," 494 U. S., at 658–659—that allow them to spend prodigious general treasury sums on campaign messages

---

they had to be formed "for the express purpose of promoting political ideas," so that their resources reflected political support rather than commercial success. *MCFL*, 479 U. S., at 264. Next, they had to have no shareholders, so that "persons connected with the organization will have no economic disincentive for disassociating with it if they disagree with its political activity." *Ibid.* Finally, they could not be "established by a business corporation or a labor union," nor "accept contributions from such entities," lest they "serv[e] as conduits for the type of direct spending that creates a threat to the political marketplace." *Ibid.*

that have "little or no correlation" with the beliefs held by actual persons, *id.,* at 660. In light of the corrupting effects such spending might have on the political process, *ibid.,* we permitted the State of Michigan to limit corporate expenditures on candidate elections to corporations' PACs, which rely on voluntary contributions and thus "reflect actual public support for the political ideals espoused by corporations," *ibid.* Notwithstanding our colleagues' insinuations that *Austin* deprived the public of general "ideas," "facts," and "knowledge," *ante,* at 38–39, the decision addressed only candidate-focused expenditures and gave the State no license to regulate corporate spending on other matters.

In the 20 years since *Austin,* we have reaffirmed its holding and rationale a number of times, see, *e.g., Beaumont,* 539 U. S., at 153–156, most importantly in *McConnell,* 540 U. S. 93, where we upheld the provision challenged here, §203 of BCRA.[62] Congress crafted §203 in response to a problem created by *Buckley.* The *Buckley*

---

[62] According to THE CHIEF JUSTICE, we are "erroneou[s]" in claiming that *McConnell* and *Beaumont* "'reaffirmed'" *Austin. Ante,* at 5. In both cases, the Court explicitly relied on *Austin* and quoted from it at length. See 540 U. S., at 204–205; 539 U. S., at 153–155, 158, 160, 163; see also *ante,* at 15 ("The holding and validity of *Austin* were essential to the reasoning of the *McConnell* majority opinion"); Brief for Appellants National Rifle Association et al., O. T. 2003, No. 02–1675, p. 21 ("*Beaumont* reaffirmed . . . the *Austin* rationale for restricting expenditures"). The *McConnell* Court did so in the teeth of vigorous protests by Justices in today's majority that *Austin* should be overruled. See *ante,* at 15 (citing relevant passages); see also *Beaumont,* 539 U. S., at 163–164 (KENNEDY, J., concurring in judgment). Both Courts also heard criticisms of *Austin* from parties or *amici.* See Brief for Appellants Chamber of Commerce of the United States et al., O. T. 2003, No. 02–1756, p. 35, n. 22; Reply Brief for Appellants/Cross-Appellees Senator Mitch McConnell et al., O. T. 2003, No. 02–1674, pp. 13–14; Brief for Pacific Legal Foundation as *Amicus Curiae* in *FEC* v. *Beaumont,* O. T. 2002, No. 02–403, *passim.* If this does not qualify as reaffirmation of a precedent, then I do not know what would.

Court had construed FECA's definition of prohibited "expenditures" narrowly to avoid any problems of constitutional vagueness, holding it applicable only to "communications that expressly advocate the election or defeat of a clearly identified candidate," 424 U. S., at 80, *i.e.*, statements containing so-called "magic words" like "'vote for,' 'elect,' 'support,' 'cast your ballot for,' 'Smith for Congress,' 'vote against,' 'defeat,' [or] 'reject,'" *id.*, at 43–44, and n. 52. After *Buckley*, corporations and unions figured out how to circumvent the limits on express advocacy by using sham "issue ads" that "eschewed the use of magic words" but nonetheless "advocate[d] the election or defeat of clearly identified federal candidates." *McConnell*, 540 U. S., at 126. "Corporations and unions spent hundreds of millions of dollars of their general funds to pay for these ads." *Id.*, at 127. Congress passed §203 to address this circumvention, prohibiting corporations and unions from using general treasury funds for electioneering communications that "refe[r] to a clearly identified candidate," whether or not those communications use the magic words. 2 U. S. C. §434(f)(3)(A)(i)(I).

When we asked in *McConnell* "whether a compelling governmental interest justifie[d]" §203, we found the question "easily answered": "We have repeatedly sustained legislation aimed at 'the corrosive and distorting effects of immense aggregations of wealth that are accumulated with the help of the corporate form and that have little or no correlation to the public's support for the corporation's political ideas.'" 540 U. S., at 205 (quoting *Austin*, 494 U. S., at 660). These precedents "represent respect for the legislative judgment that the special characteristics of the corporate structure require particularly careful regulation." 540 U. S., at 205 (internal quotation marks omitted). "Moreover, recent cases have recognized that certain restrictions on corporate electoral involvement permissibly hedge against "'circumvention of [valid] contribution limits."'" *Ibid.* (quoting *Beaumont,* 539 U. S., at 155, in turn quoting *FEC* v. *Colorado Republican Federal Campaign Comm.,* 533 U. S. 431, 456, and n. 18 (2001) *(Colorado II);* alteration in original). BCRA, we found, is faithful to the compelling governmental interests in "'preserving the integrity of the electoral process, preventing corruption, . . . sustaining the active, alert responsibility of the individual citizen in a democracy for the wise conduct of the government,'" and maintaining "'the individual citizen's confidence in government.'" 540 U. S., at 206–207, n. 88 (quoting *Bellotti,* 435 U. S., at 788–789; some internal quotation marks and brackets omitted). What made the answer even easier than it might have been otherwise was the option to form PACs, which give corporations, at the least, "a constitutionally sufficient opportunity to engage in" independent expenditures. 540 U. S., at 203.

3. *Buckley and Bellotti*

Against this extensive background of congressional regulation of corporate campaign spending, and our repeated affirmation of this regulation as constitutionally sound, the majority dismisses *Austin* as "a significant departure from ancient First Amendment principles," *ante,* at 1 (internal quotation marks omitted). How does the majority attempt to justify this claim? Selected passages from two cases, *Buckley,* 424 U. S. 1, and *Bellotti,* 435 U. S. 765, do all of the work. In the Court's view, *Buckley* and *Bellotti* decisively rejected the possibility of distinguishing corporations from natural persons in the 1970's; it just so happens that in every single case in which the Court has reviewed campaign finance legislation in the decades since, the majority failed to grasp this truth. The Federal Congress and dozens of state legislatures, we now know, have been similarly deluded.

The majority emphasizes *Buckley*'s statement that

"'[t]he concept that government may restrict the speech of some elements of our society in order to enhance the relative voice of others is wholly foreign to the First Amendment.'" *Ante*, at 33 (quoting 424 U. S., at 48–49); *ante*, at 8 (opinion of ROBERTS, C. J.).   But this elegant phrase cannot bear the weight that our colleagues have placed on it.   For one thing, the Constitution does, in fact, permit numerous "restrictions on the speech of some in order to prevent a few from drowning out the many": for example, restrictions on ballot access and on legislators' floor time. *Nixon* v. *Shrink Missouri Government PAC*, 528 U. S. 377, 402 (2000) (BREYER, J., concurring).   For another, the *Buckley* Court used this line in evaluating "the ancillary governmental interest in equalizing the relative ability of individuals and groups to influence the outcome of elections."   424 U. S., at 48.   It is not apparent why this is relevant to the case before us.   The majority suggests that *Austin* rests on the foreign concept of speech equalization, *ante*, at 34; *ante*, at 8–10 (opinion of ROBERTS, C. J.), but we made it clear in *Austin* (as in several cases before and since) that a restriction on the way corporations spend their money is no mere exercise in disfavoring the voice of some elements of our society in preference to others. Indeed, we *expressly* ruled that the compelling interest supporting Michigan's statute was not one of "'equaliz[ing] the relative influence of speakers on elections,'" *Austin*, 494 U. S., at 660 (quoting *id.*, at 705 (KENNEDY, J., dissenting)), but rather the need to confront the distinctive corrupting potential of corporate electoral advocacy financed by general treasury dollars, *id.*, at 659–660.

For that matter, it should go without saying that when we made this statement in *Buckley*, we could not have been casting doubt on the restriction on corporate expenditures in candidate elections, which had not been challenged as "foreign to the First Amendment," *ante*, at 33 (quoting *Buckley*, 424 U. S., at 49), or for any other reason.

Buckley's independent expenditure analysis was focused on a very different statutory provision, 18 U. S. C. §608(e)(1) (1970 ed., Supp. V). It is implausible to think, as the majority suggests, *ante*, at 29–30, that *Buckley* covertly invalidated FECA's separate corporate and union campaign expenditure restriction, §610 (now codified at 2 U. S. C. §441b), even though that restriction had been on the books for decades before *Buckley* and would remain on the books, undisturbed, for decades after.

The case on which the majority places even greater weight than *Buckley*, however, is *Bellotti*, 435 U. S. 765, claiming it "could not have been clearer" that *Bellotti*'s holding forbade distinctions between corporate and individual expenditures like the one at issue here, *ante*, at 30. The Court's reliance is odd. The only thing about *Bellotti* that could not be clearer is that it declined to adopt the majority's position. *Bellotti* ruled, in an explicit limitation on the scope of its holding, that "our consideration of a corporation's right to speak on issues of general public interest implies no comparable right in the quite different context of participation in a political campaign for election to public office." 435 U. S., at 788, n. 26; see also *id.*, at 787–788 (acknowledging that the interests in preserving public confidence in Government and protecting dissenting shareholders may be "weighty . . . in the context of partisan candidate elections"). *Bellotti*, in other words, did not touch the question presented in *Austin* and *McConnell*, and the opinion squarely disavowed the proposition for which the majority cites it.

The majority attempts to explain away the distinction *Bellotti* drew—between general corporate speech and campaign speech intended to promote or prevent the election of specific candidates for office—as inconsistent with the rest of the opinion and with *Buckley*. *Ante*, at 31, 42–44. Yet the basis for this distinction is perfectly coherent: The anticorruption interests that animate regulations of corporate participation in candidate elections, the "importance" of which "has never been doubted," 435 U. S., at 788, n. 26, do not apply equally to regulations of corporate participation in referenda. A referendum cannot owe a political debt to a corporation, seek to curry favor with a corporation, or fear the corporation's retaliation. Cf. *Austin*, 494 U. S., at 678 (STEVENS, J., concurring); *Citizens Against Rent Control/Coalition for Fair Housing* v. *Berkeley*, 454 U. S. 290, 299 (1981). The majority likewise overlooks the fact that, over the past 30 years, our cases have repeatedly recognized the candidate/issue distinction. See, *e.g., Austin*, 494 U. S., at 659; *NCPAC*, 470 U. S., at 495–496; *FCC* v. *League of Women Voters of Cal.*, 468 U. S. 364, 371, n. 9 (1984); *NRWC*, 459 U. S., at 210, n. 7. The Court's critique of *Bellotti*'s footnote 26 puts it in the strange position of trying to elevate *Bellotti* to canonical status, while simultaneously disparaging a critical piece of its analysis as unsupported and irreconcilable with *Buckley*. *Bellotti*, apparently, is both the font of all wisdom and internally incoherent.

The *Bellotti* Court confronted a dramatically different factual situation from the one that confronts us in this case: a state statute that barred business corporations' expenditures on some referenda but not others. Specifically, the statute barred a business corporation "from making contributions or expenditures 'for the purpose of . . . influencing or affecting the vote on any question submitted to the voters, other than one materially affecting any of the property, business or assets of the corporation,'" 435 U. S., at 768 (quoting Mass. Gen. Laws Ann., ch. 55, §8 (West Supp. 1977); alteration in original), and it went so far as to provide that referenda related to income taxation would not "'be deemed materially to affect the property, business or assets of the corporation,'" 435 U. S., at 768. As might be guessed, the legislature had enacted this statute in order to limit corporate speech on a proposed state constitutional amendment to authorize a graduated income tax. The statute was a transparent attempt to prevent corporations from spending money to defeat this amendment, which was favored by a majority of legislators but had been repeatedly rejected by the voters. See *id.*, at 769–770, and n. 3. We said that "where, as here, the legislature's suppression of speech suggests an attempt to give one side of a debatable public question an advantage in expressing its views to the people, the First Amendment is plainly offended." *Id.*, at 785–786 (footnote omitted).

Bellotti thus involved a *viewpoint-discriminatory* statute, created to effect a particular policy outcome. Even Justice Rehnquist, in dissent, had to acknowledge that "a very persuasive argument could be made that the [Massachusetts Legislature], desiring to impose a personal income tax but more than once defeated in that desire by the combination of the Commonwealth's referendum provision and corporate expenditures in opposition to such a tax, simply decided to muzzle corporations on this sort of issue so that it could succeed in its desire." *Id.*, at 827, n. 6. To make matters worse, the law at issue did not make any allowance for corporations to spend money through PACs. *Id.*, at 768, n. 2 (opinion of the Court). This really was a complete ban on a specific, preidentified subject. See *MCFL*, 479 U. S., at 259, n. 12 (stating that 2 U. S. C. §441b's expenditure restriction "is *of course distinguishable* from the complete foreclosure of any opportunity for political speech that we invalidated in the state referendum context in . . . *Bellotti*" (emphasis added)).

The majority grasps a quotational straw from *Bellotti*, that speech does not fall entirely outside the protection of the First Amendment merely because it comes from a corporation. *Ante*, at 30–31. Of course not, but no one suggests the contrary and neither *Austin* nor *McConnell* held otherwise. They held that even though the expenditures at issue were subject to First Amendment scrutiny, the restrictions on those expenditures were justified by a compelling state interest. See *McConnell*, 540 U. S., at 205; *Austin*, 494 U. S., at 658, 660. We acknowledged in *Bellotti* that numerous "interests of the highest importance" can justify campaign finance regulation. 435 U. S., at 788–789. But we found no evidence that these interests were served by the Massachusetts law. *Id.*, at 789. We left open the possibility that our decision might have been different if there had been "record or legislative findings that corporate advocacy threatened imminently to undermine democratic processes, thereby denigrating rather than serving First Amendment interests." *Ibid.*

Austin and *McConnell*, then, sit perfectly well with *Bellotti*. Indeed, all six Members of the *Austin* majority had been on the Court at the time of *Bellotti*, and none so much as hinted in *Austin* that they saw any tension between the decisions. The difference between the cases is not that *Austin* and *McConnell* rejected First Amendment protection for corporations whereas *Bellotti* accepted it. The difference is that the statute at issue in *Bellotti* smacked of viewpoint discrimination, targeted one class of corporations, and provided no PAC option; and the State has a greater interest in regulating independent corporate expenditures on candidate elections than on referenda, because in a functioning democracy the public must have faith that its representatives owe their positions to the people, not to the corporations with the deepest pockets.

*   *   *

In sum, over the course of the past century Congress has demonstrated a recurrent need to regulate corporate participation in candidate elections to "'[p]reserv[e] the integrity of the electoral process, preven[t] corruption, . . . sustai[n] the active, alert responsibility of the individual citizen,'" protect the expressive interests of shareholders, and "'[p]reserv[e] . . . the individual citizen's confidence in government.'"   *McConnell*, 540 U. S., at 206–207, n. 88 (quoting *Bellotti*, 435 U. S., at 788–789; first alteration in original).   These understandings provided the combined impetus behind the Tillman Act in 1907, see *Automobile Workers*, 352 U. S., at 570–575, the Taft-Hartley Act in 1947, see *WRTL*, 551 U. S., at 511 (Souter, J., dissenting), FECA in 1971, see *NRWC*, 459 U. S., at 209–210, and BCRA in 2002, see *McConnell*, 540 U. S., at 126–132. Continuously for over 100 years, this line of "[c]ampaign finance reform has been a series of reactions to docu-mented threats to electoral integrity obvious to any voter, posed by large sums of money from corporate or union treasuries." *WRTL*, 551 U. S., at 522 (Souter, J., dissent-ing).   Time and again, we have recognized these realities in approving measures that Congress and the States have taken.   None of the cases the majority cites is to the con-trary.   The only thing new about *Austin* was the dissent, with its stunning failure to appreciate the legitimacy of interests recognized in the name of democratic integrity since the days of the Progressives.

IV

Having explained why this is not an appropriate case in which to revisit *Austin* and *McConnell* and why these decisions sit perfectly well with "First Amendment princi-ples," *ante*, at 1, 48, I come at last to the interests that are at stake.   The majority recognizes that *Austin* and *McConnell* may be defended on anticorruption, antidistor-tion, and shareholder protection rationales.   *Ante*, at 32–46.   It badly errs both in explaining the nature of these rationales, which overlap and complement each other, and in applying them to the case at hand.

The Anticorruption Interest

Undergirding the majority's approach to the merits is the claim that the only "sufficiently important governmental interest in preventing corruption or the appearance of corruption" is one that is "limited to *quid pro quo* corruption." *Ante*, at 43. This is the same "crabbed view of corruption" that was espoused by Justice Kennedy in *McConnell* and squarely rejected by the Court in that case. 540 U. S., at 152. While it is true that we have not always spoken about corruption in a clear or consistent voice, the approach taken by the majority cannot be right, in my judgment. It disregards our constitutional history and the fundamental demands of a democratic society.

On numerous occasions we have recognized Congress' legitimate interest in preventing the money that is spent on elections from exerting an "'undue influence on an officeholder's judgment'" and from creating "'the appearance of such influence,'" beyond the sphere of *quid pro quo* relationships. *Id.*, at 150; see also, *e.g., id.*, at 143–144, 152–154; *Colorado II*, 533 U. S., at 441; *Shrink Missouri*, 528 U. S., at 389. Corruption can take many forms. Bribery may be the paradigm case. But the difference between selling a vote and selling access is a matter of degree, not kind. And selling access is not qualitatively different from giving special preference to those who spent money on one's behalf. Corruption operates along a spectrum, and the majority's apparent belief that *quid pro quo* arrangements can be neatly demarcated from other improper influences does not accord with the theory or reality of politics. It certainly does not accord with the record Congress developed in passing BCRA, a record that stands as a remarkable testament to the energy and ingenuity with which corporations, unions, lobbyists, and politicians may go about scratching each other's backs—and which amply supported Congress' determination to target a limited set of especially destructive practices.

The District Court that adjudicated the initial challenge to BCRA pored over this record. In a careful analysis, Judge Kollar-Kotelly made numerous findings about the

corrupting consequences of corporate and union independent expenditures in the years preceding BCRA's passage.
See *McConnell*, 251 F. Supp. 2d, at 555–560, 622–625; see
also *id.*, at 804–805, 813, n. 143 (Leon, J.) (indicating
agreement). As summarized in her own words:

> "The factual findings of the Court illustrate that
> corporations and labor unions routinely notify Mem-
> bers of Congress as soon as they air electioneering
> communications relevant to the Members' elections.
> The record also indicates that Members express ap-
> preciation to organizations for the airing of these elec-
> tion-related advertisements.   Indeed, Members of
> Congress are particularly grateful when negative is-
> sue advertisements are run by these organizations,
> leaving the candidates free to run positive advertise-
> ments and be seen as 'above the fray.' Political con-
> sultants testify that campaigns are quite aware of
> who is running advertisements on the candidate's be-
> half, when they are being run, and where they are be-
> ing run. Likewise, a prominent lobbyist testifies that
> these organizations use issue advocacy as a means to
> influence various Members of Congress.

> "The Findings also demonstrate that Members of
> Congress seek to have corporations and unions run
> these advertisements on their behalf. The Findings
> show that Members suggest that corporations or indi-
> viduals make donations to interest groups with the
> understanding that the money contributed to these
> groups will assist the Member in a campaign. After
> the election, these organizations often seek credit for
> their support. . . . Finally, a large majority of Ameri-
> cans (80%) are of the view that corporations and other
> organizations that engage in electioneering communi-
> cations, which benefit specific elected officials, receive
> special consideration from those officials when matters

arise that affect these corporations and organizations."
Id., at 623–624 (citations and footnote omitted).

Many of the relationships of dependency found by Judge
Kollar-Kotelly seemed to have a *quid pro quo* basis, but
other arrangements were more subtle.   Her analysis
shows the great difficulty in delimiting the precise scope of
the *quid pro quo* category, as well as the adverse consequences that *all* such arrangements may have.   There are
threats of corruption that are far more destructive to a
democratic society than the odd bribe.   Yet the majority's
understanding of corruption would leave lawmakers impo-
tent to address all but the most discrete abuses.

Our "undue influence" cases have allowed the American
people to cast a wider net through legislative experiments
designed to ensure, to some minimal extent, "that officeholders will decide issues . . . on the merits or the desires
of their constituencies," and not "according to the wishes of
those who have made large financial contributions"—or
expenditures—"valued by the officeholder." *McConnell,*
540 U. S., at 153.[63]   When private interests are seen to
exert outsized control over officeholders solely on account
of the money spent on (or withheld from) their campaigns,
the result can depart so thoroughly "from what is pure or

---

[63] Cf. *Nixon* v. *Shrink Missouri Government PAC,* 528 U. S. 377, 389
(2000) (recognizing "the broader threat from politicians too compliant
with the wishes of large contributors").   Though discrete in scope, these
experiments must impose some meaningful limits if they are to have a
chance at functioning effectively and preserving the public's trust.
"Even if it occurs only occasionally, the potential for such undue influence is manifest.   And unlike straight cash-for-votes transactions, such
corruption is neither easily detected nor practical to criminalize."
McConnell, 540 U. S., at 153.   There should be nothing controversial
about the proposition that the influence being targeted is "undue."   In a
democracy, officeholders should not make public decisions with the aim
of placating a financial benefactor, except to the extent that the benefactor is seen as representative of a larger constituency or its arguments are seen as especially persuasive.

correct" in the conduct of Government, Webster's Third
New International Dictionary 512 (1966) (defining "corruption"), that it amounts to a "subversion . . . of the electoral process," *Automobile Workers*, 352 U. S., at 575. At
stake in the legislative efforts to address this threat is
therefore not only the legitimacy and quality of Government but also the public's faith therein, not only "the
capacity of this democracy to represent its constituents
[but also] the confidence of its citizens in their capacity to
govern themselves," *WRTL*, 551 U. S., at 507 (Souter, J.,
dissenting). "Take away Congress' authority to regulate
the appearance of undue influence and 'the cynical assumption that large donors call the tune could jeopardize
the willingness of voters to take part in democratic governance.'" *McConnell*, 540 U. S., at 144 (quoting *Shrink
Missouri*, 528 U. S., at 390).[64]

The cluster of interrelated interests threatened by such
undue influence and its appearance has been well captured under the rubric of "democratic integrity." *WRTL*,
551 U. S., at 522 (Souter, J., dissenting). This value has
underlined a century of state and federal efforts to regulate the role of corporations in the electoral process.[65]

---

[64] The majority declares by fiat that the appearance of undue influence by high-spending corporations "will not cause the electorate to lose
faith in our democracy." *Ante*, at 44. The electorate itself has consistently indicated otherwise, both in opinion polls, see *McConnell v. FEC*,
251 F. Supp. 2d 176, 557–558, 623–624 (DC 2003) (opinion of Kollar-
Kotelly, J.), and in the laws its representatives have passed, and our
colleagues have no basis for elevating their own optimism into a tenet
of constitutional law.

[65] Quite distinct from the interest in preventing improper influences
on the electoral process, I have long believed that "a number of [other]
purposes, both legitimate and substantial, may justify the imposition of
reasonable limitations on the expenditures permitted during the course
of any single campaign." *Davis v. FEC*, 554 U. S. ___, ___ (2008) (slip
op., at 3) (opinion concurring in part and dissenting in part). In my
judgment, such limitations may be justified to the extent they are
tailored to "improving the quality of the exposition of ideas" that voters

Unlike the majority's myopic focus on *quid pro quo* scenarios and the free-floating "First Amendment principles" on which it rests so much weight, *ante*, at 1, 48, this broader understanding of corruption has deep roots in the Nation's history. "During debates on the earliest [campaign finance] reform acts, the terms 'corruption' and 'undue influence' were used nearly interchangeably." Pasquale, Reclaiming Egalitarianism in the Political Theory of Campaign Finance Reform, 2008 U. Ill. L. Rev. 599, 601. Long before *Buckley*, we appreciated that "[t]o say that Congress is without power to pass appropriate legislation to safeguard . . . an election from the improper use of money to influence the result is to deny to the nation in a vital particular the power of self protection." *Burroughs* v. *United States*, 290 U. S. 534, 545 (1934). And whereas we have no evidence to support the notion that the Framers would have wanted corporations to have the same rights as natural persons in the electoral context, we have ample evidence to suggest that they would have been appalled by the evidence of corruption that Congress unearthed in developing BCRA and that the Court today discounts to irrelevance. It is fair to say that "[t]he Framers were obsessed with corruption," Teachout 348, which they understood to encompass the dependency of public officeholders on private interests, see *id.*, at 373–374; see also *Randall*, 548 U. S., at 280 (STEVENS, J., dissenting). They discussed corruption "more often in the Constitutional Convention than factions, violence, or instability." Teachout 352. When they brought our consti-

---

receive, *ibid.*, "free[ing] candidates and their staffs from the interminable burden of fundraising," *ibid.* (internal quotation marks omitted), and "protect[ing] equal access to the political arena," *Randall* v. *Sorrell*, 548 U. S. 230, 278 (2006) (STEVENS, J., dissenting) (internal quotation marks omitted). I continue to adhere to these beliefs, but they have not been briefed by the parties or *amici* in this case, and their soundness is immaterial to its proper disposition.

tutional order into being, the Framers had their minds trained on a threat to republican self-government that this Court has lost sight of.

Quid Pro Quo *Corruption*

There is no need to take my side in the debate over the scope of the anticorruption interest to see that the Court's merits holding is wrong.   Even under the majority's "crabbed view of corruption," *McConnell*, 540 U. S., at 152, the Government should not lose this case.

"The importance of the governmental interest in preventing [corruption through the creation of political debts] has never been doubted." *Bellotti*, 435 U. S., at 788, n. 26. Even in the cases that have construed the anticorruption interest most narrowly, we have never suggested that such *quid pro quo* debts must take the form of outright vote buying or bribes, which have long been distinct crimes. Rather, they encompass the myriad ways in which outside parties may induce an officeholder to confer a legislative benefit in direct response to, or anticipation of, some outlay of money the parties have made or will make on behalf of the officeholder. See *McConnell*, 540 U. S., at 143 ("We have not limited [the anticorruption] interest to the elimination of cash-for-votes exchanges.   In *Buckley*, we expressly rejected the argument that antibribery laws provided a less restrictive alternative to FECA's contribution limits, noting that such laws 'deal[t] with only the most blatant and specific attempts of those with money to influence governmental action'" (quoting 424 U. S., at 28; alteration in original)).   It has likewise never been doubted that "[o]f almost equal concern as the danger of actual *quid pro quo* arrangements is the impact of the appearance of corruption."   *Id.*, at 27.   Congress may "legitimately conclude that the avoidance of the appearance of improper influence is also critical . . . if confidence in the system of representative Government is not to be eroded to a disastrous extent." *Ibid.* (internal quotation marks omitted; alteration in original). A democracy cannot function effectively when its constituent members believe laws are being bought and sold.

In theory, our colleagues accept this much. As applied to BCRA §203, however, they conclude "[t]he anticorruption interest is not sufficient to displace the speech here in question." *Ante*, at 41.

Although the Court suggests that *Buckley* compels its conclusion, *ante*, at 40–44, *Buckley* cannot sustain this reading. It is true that, in evaluating FECA's ceiling on independent expenditures by all persons, the *Buckley* Court found the governmental interest in preventing corruption "inadequate." 424 U. S., at 45. But *Buckley* did not evaluate corporate expenditures specifically, nor did it rule out the possibility that a future Court might find otherwise. The opinion reasoned that an expenditure limitation covering only express advocacy (*i.e.*, magic words) would likely be ineffectual, *ibid.*, a problem that Congress tackled in BCRA, and it concluded that "the independent advocacy restricted by [FECA §608(e)(1)] *does not presently appear* to pose dangers of real or apparent corruption comparable to those identified with large campaign contributions," *id.,* at 46 (emphasis added). *Buckley* expressly contemplated that an anticorruption rationale might justify restrictions on independent expenditures at a later date, "because it may be that, in some circumstances, 'large independent expenditures pose the same dangers of actual or apparent *quid pro quo* arrangements as do large contributions.'" *WRTL*, 551 U. S., at 478 (opinion of ROBERTS, C. J.) (quoting *Buckley*, 424 U. S., at 45). Certainly *Buckley* did not foreclose this possibility with respect to electioneering communications made with corporate general treasury funds, an issue the Court had no occasion to consider.

The *Austin* Court did not rest its holding on *quid pro*

quo corruption, as it found the broader corruption impli- cated by the antidistortion and shareholder protection rationales a sufficient basis for Michigan's restriction on corporate electioneering. 494 U. S., at 658–660. Concur- ring in that opinion, I took the position that "the danger of either the fact, or the appearance, of *quid pro quo* rela- tionships [also] provides an adequate justification for state regulation" of these independent expenditures. *Id.*, at 678. I did not see this position as inconsistent with *Buckley*'s analysis of individual expenditures. Corporations, as a class, tend to be more attuned to the complexities of the legislative process and more directly affected by tax and appropriations measures that receive little public scrutiny; they also have vastly more money with which to try to buy access and votes. See Supp. Brief for Appellee 17 (stating that the Fortune 100 companies earned revenues of $13.1 trillion during the last election cycle). Business corpora- tions must engage the political process in instrumental terms if they are to maximize shareholder value. The unparalleled resources, professional lobbyists, and single- minded focus they bring to this effort, I believed, make *quid pro quo* corruption and its appearance inherently more likely when they (or their conduits or trade groups) spend unrestricted sums on elections.

It is with regret rather than satisfaction that I can now say that time has borne out my concerns. The legislative and judicial proceedings relating to BCRA generated a substantial body of evidence suggesting that, as corpora- tions grew more and more adept at crafting "issue ads" to help or harm a particular candidate, these nominally independent expenditures began to corrupt the political process in a very direct sense. The sponsors of these ads were routinely granted special access after the campaign was over; "candidates and officials knew who their friends were," *McConnell*, 540 U. S., at 129. Many corporate independent expenditures, it seemed, had become essentially interchangeable with direct contributions in their capacity to generate *quid pro quo* arrangements. In an age in which money and television ads are the coin of the campaign realm, it is hardly surprising that corporations deployed these ads to curry favor with, and to gain influence over, public officials.

The majority appears to think it decisive that the BCRA record does not contain "direct examples of votes being exchanged for ... expenditures." *Ante*, at 45 (internal quotation marks omitted). It would have been quite remarkable if Congress had created a record detailing such behavior by its own Members. Proving that a specific vote was exchanged for a specific expenditure has always been next to impossible: Elected officials have diverse motivations, and no one will acknowledge that he sold a vote. Yet, even if "[i]ngratiation and access ... are not corruption" themselves, *ibid.*, they are necessary prerequisites to it; they can create both the opportunity for, and the appearance of, *quid pro quo* arrangements. The influx of unlimited corporate money into the electoral realm also creates new opportunities for the mirror image of *quid pro quo* deals: threats, both explicit and implicit. Starting today, corporations with large war chests to deploy on electioneering may find democratically elected bodies becoming much more attuned to their interests. The majority both misreads the facts and draws the wrong conclusions when it suggests that the BCRA record provides "only scant evidence that independent expenditures ... ingratiate," and that, "in any event," none of it matters. *Ibid.*

In her analysis of the record, Judge Kollar-Kotelly documented the pervasiveness of this ingratiation and explained its significance under the majority's own touchstone for defining the scope of the anticorruption rationale, *Buckley*. See *McConnell*, 251 F. Supp. 2d, at 555–560, 622–625. Witnesses explained how political parties and candidates used corporate independent expenditures to circumvent FECA's "hard-money" limitations. See, *e.g., id.,* at 478–479. One former Senator candidly admitted to the District Court that "'[c]andidates whose campaigns benefit from [phony "issue ads"] greatly appreciate the help of these groups. In fact, Members will also be favorably disposed to those who finance these groups when they later seek access to discuss pending legislation.'" *Id.,* at 556 (quoting declaration of Sen. Dale Bumpers). One prominent lobbyist went so far as to state, in uncontroverted testimony, that "'unregulated expenditures— whether soft money donations to the parties or issue ad campaigns—can sometimes generate *far more* influence than direct campaign contributions.'" *Ibid.* (quoting declaration of Wright Andrews; emphasis added). In sum, Judge Kollar-Kotelly found, "[t]he record powerfully demonstrates that electioneering communications paid for with the general treasury funds of labor unions and corporations endears those entities to elected officials in a way that could be perceived by the public as corrupting." *Id.,* at 622–623. She concluded that the Government's interest in preventing the appearance of corruption, as that concept was defined in *Buckley,* was itself sufficient to uphold BCRA §203. 251 F. Supp. 2d, at 622–625. Judge Leon agreed. See *id.,* at 804–805 (dissenting only with respect to the Wellstone Amendment's coverage of *MCFL* corporations).

When the *McConnell* Court affirmed the judgment of the District Court regarding §203, we did not rest our holding on a narrow notion of *quid pro quo* corruption. Instead we relied on the governmental interest in combating the unique forms of corruption threatened by corporations, as recognized in *Austin*'s antidistortion and shareholder protection rationales, 540 U. S., at 205 (citing *Austin,* 494 U. S., at 660), as well as the interest in preventing circumvention of contribution limits, 540 U. S., at 128–129,

205, 206, n. 88. Had we felt constrained by the view of
today's Court that *quid pro quo* corruption and its appearance are the only interests that count in this field, *ante*, at
32–46, we of course would have looked closely at that
issue. And as the analysis by Judge Kollar-Kotelly reflects, it is a very real possibility that we would have found
one or both of those interests satisfied and §203 appropriately tailored to them.

The majority's rejection of the *Buckley* anticorruption
rationale on the ground that independent corporate expenditures "do not give rise to [*quid pro quo*] corruption or
the appearance of corruption," *ante*, at 42, is thus unfair
as well as unreasonable. Congress and outside experts
have generated significant evidence corroborating this
rationale, and the only reason we do not have any of the
relevant materials before us is that the Government had
no reason to develop a record at trial for a facial challenge
the plaintiff had abandoned. The Court cannot both
sua sponte choose to relitigate *McConnell* on appeal and
then complain that the Government has failed to substantiate its case. If our colleagues were really serious about
the interest in preventing *quid pro quo* corruption, they
would remand to the District Court with instructions to
commence evidentiary proceedings.[66]

The insight that even technically independent expendi-

---

[66] In fact, the notion that the "electioneering communications" covered
by §203 can breed *quid pro quo* corruption or the appearance of such
corruption has only become more plausible since we decided *McConnell*.
Recall that THE CHIEF JUSTICE's controlling opinion in *WRTL* subsequently limited BCRA's definition of "electioneering communications"
to those that are "susceptible of no reasonable interpretation other than
as an appeal to vote for or against a specific candidate." 551 U. S., at
470. The upshot was that after *WRTL*, a corporate or union expenditure could be regulated under §203 only if everyone would understand
it as an endorsement of or attack on a particular candidate for office. It
does not take much imagination to perceive why this type of advocacy
might be especially apt to look like or amount to a deal or a threat.

tures can be corrupting in much the same way as direct contributions is bolstered by our decision last year in *Caperton* v. *A. T. Massey Coal Co.,* 556 U. S. ___ (2009). In that case, Don Blankenship, the chief executive officer of a corporation with a lawsuit pending before the West Virginia high court, spent large sums on behalf of a particular candidate, Brent Benjamin, running for a seat on that court. "In addition to contributing the $1,000 statutory maximum to Benjamin's campaign committee, Blankenship donated almost $2.5 million to 'And For The Sake Of The Kids,'" a §527 corporation that ran ads targeting Benjamin's opponent. *Id.,* at ___ (slip op., at 2). "This was not all. Blankenship spent, in addition, just over $500,000 on independent expenditures . . . '"to support . . . Brent Benjamin."'" *Id.,* at ___ (slip op., at 2–3) (second alteration in original). Applying its common sense, this Court accepted petitioners' argument that Blankenship's "pivotal role in getting Justice Benjamin elected created a constitutionally intolerable probability of actual bias" when Benjamin later declined to recuse himself from the appeal by Blankenship's corporation. *Id.,* at ___ (slip op., at 11). "Though n[o] . . . bribe or criminal influence" was involved, we recognized that "Justice Benjamin would nevertheless feel a debt of gratitude to Blankenship for his extraordinary efforts to get him elected." *Ibid.* "The difficulties of inquiring into actual bias," we further noted, "simply underscore the need for objective rules," *id.,* at ___ (slip op., at 13)—rules which will perforce turn on the appearance of bias rather than its actual existence.

In *Caperton,* then, we accepted the premise that, at least in some circumstances, independent expenditures on candidate elections will raise an intolerable specter of *quid pro quo* corruption. Indeed, this premise struck the Court as so intuitive that it repeatedly referred to Blankenship's spending on behalf of Benjamin—spending that consisted of 99.97% independent expenditures ($3 million) and 0.03% direct contributions ($1,000)—as a "contribution." See, *e.g., id.,* at ___ (slip op., at 1) ("The basis for the [recusal] motion was that the justice had received campaign contributions in an extraordinary amount from" Blankenship); *id.,* at ___ (slip op., at 3) (referencing "Blankenship's $3 million in contributions"); *id.,* at ___ (slip op., at 14) ("Blankenship contributed some $3 million to unseat the incumbent and replace him with Benjamin"); *id.,* at ___ (slip op., at 15) ("Blankenship's campaign contributions . . . had a significant and disproportionate influence on the electoral outcome"). The reason the Court so thoroughly conflated expenditures and contributions, one assumes, is that it realized that some expenditures may be functionally equivalent to contributions in the way they influence the outcome of a race, the way they are interpreted by the candidates and the public, and the way they taint the decisions that the officeholder thereafter takes.

Caperton is illuminating in several additional respects. It underscores the old insight that, on account of the extreme difficulty of proving corruption, "prophylactic measures, reaching some [campaign spending] not corrupt in purpose or effect, [may be] nonetheless required to guard against corruption." *Buckley,* 424 U. S., at 30; see also *Shrink Missouri,* 528 U. S., at 392, n. 5. It underscores that "certain restrictions on corporate electoral involvement" may likewise be needed to "hedge against circumvention of valid contribution limits." *McConnell,* 540 U. S., at 205 (internal quotation marks and brackets omitted); see also *Colorado II,* 533 U. S., at 456 ("[A]ll Members of the Court agree that circumvention is a valid theory of corruption"). It underscores that for-profit corporations associated with electioneering communications will often prefer to use nonprofit conduits with "misleading names," such as And For The Sake Of The Kids, "to conceal their identity" as the sponsor of those communications, thereby frustrating the utility of disclosure laws. *McConnell*, 540 U. S., at 128; see also *id.*, at 196–197.

And it underscores that the consequences of today's holding will not be limited to the legislative or executive context. The majority of the States select their judges through popular elections. At a time when concerns about the conduct of judicial elections have reached a fever pitch, see, *e.g.,* O'Connor, Justice for Sale, Wall St. Journal, Nov. 15, 2007, p. A25; Brief for Justice at Stake et al. as *Amici Curiae* 2, the Court today unleashes the floodgates of corporate and union general treasury spending in these races. Perhaps "*Caperton* motions" will catch some of the worst abuses. This will be small comfort to those States that, after today, may no longer have the ability to place modest limits on corporate electioneering even if they believe such limits to be critical to maintaining the integrity of their judicial systems.

Deference and Incumbent Self-Protection

Rather than show any deference to a coordinate branch of Government, the majority thus rejects the anticorruption rationale without serious analysis.[67] Today's opinion provides no clear rationale for being so dismissive of Congress, but the prior individual opinions on which it relies have offered one: the incentives of the legislators who passed BCRA. Section 203, our colleagues have suggested, may be little more than "an incumbency protection plan," *McConnell*, 540 U. S., at 306 (KENNEDY, J., concurring in judgment in part and dissenting in part); see also *id.*, at 249–250, 260–263 (SCALIA, J., concurring in part, concurring in judgment in part, and dissenting in part), a dis-

---

[67] "We must give weight" and "due deference" to Congress' efforts to dispel corruption, the Court states at one point. *Ante*, at 45. It is unclear to me what these maxims mean, but as applied by the Court they clearly do not entail "deference" in any normal sense of that term.

reputable attempt at legislative self-dealing rather than an earnest effort to facilitate First Amendment values and safeguard the legitimacy of our political system. This possibility, the Court apparently believes, licenses it to run roughshod over Congress' handiwork.

In my view, we should instead start by acknowledging that "Congress surely has both wisdom and experience in these matters that is far superior to ours." *Colorado Republican Federal Campaign Comm. v. FEC*, 518 U. S. 604, 650 (1996) (STEVENS, J., dissenting). Many of our campaign finance precedents explicitly and forcefully affirm the propriety of such presumptive deference. See, *e.g., McConnell*, 540 U. S., at 158; *Beaumont*, 539 U. S., at 155–156; *NRWC*, 459 U. S., at 209–210. Moreover, "[j]udicial deference is particularly warranted where, as here, we deal with a congressional judgment that has remained essentially unchanged throughout a century of careful legislative adjustment." *Beaumont*, 539 U. S., at 162, n. 9 (internal quotation marks omitted); cf. *Shrink Missouri,* 528 U. S., at 391 ("The quantum of empirical evidence needed to satisfy heightened judicial scrutiny of legislative judgments will vary up or down with the novelty and plausibility of the justification raised"). In America, incumbent legislators pass the laws that govern campaign finance, just like all other laws. To apply a level of scrutiny that effectively bars them from regulating electioneering whenever there is the faintest whiff of self-interest, is to deprive them of the ability to regulate electioneering.

This is not to say that deference would be appropriate if there were a solid basis for believing that a legislative action was motivated by the desire to protect incumbents or that it will degrade the competitiveness of the electoral process.[68] See *League of United Latin American Citizens*

---

[68]JUSTICE BREYER has suggested that we strike the balance as fol-

v. *Perry*, 548 U. S. 399, 447 (2006) (STEVENS, J., concurring in part and dissenting in part); *Vieth* v. *Jubelirer*, 541 U. S. 267, 317 (2004) (STEVENS, J., dissenting). Along with our duty to balance competing constitutional concerns, we have a vital role to play in ensuring that elections remain at least minimally open, fair, and competitive. But it is the height of recklessness to dismiss Congress' years of bipartisan deliberation and its reasoned judgment on this basis, without first confirming that the statute in question was intended to be, or will function as, a restraint on electoral competition. "Absent record evidence of invidious discrimination against challengers as a class, a court should generally be hesitant to invalidate legislation which on its face imposes evenhanded restrictions." *Buckley*, 424 U. S., at 31.

We have no record evidence from which to conclude that BCRA §203, or any of the dozens of state laws that the Court today calls into question, reflects or fosters such invidious discrimination. Our colleagues have opined that "'*any* restriction upon a type of campaign speech that is equally available to challengers and incumbents tends to favor incumbents.'" *McConnell*, 540 U. S., at 249 (opinion of SCALIA, J.). This kind of airy speculation could easily be turned on its head. The electioneering prohibited by §203 might well tend to favor incumbents, because incumbents have pre-existing relationships with corporations and unions, and groups that wish to procure legislative benefits may tend to support the candidate who, as a sitting officeholder, is already in a position to dispense benefits and is statistically likely to retain office. If a corporation's goal is to induce officeholders to do its bidding, the corpo-

---

lows: "We should defer to [the legislature's] political judgment that unlimited spending threatens the integrity of the electoral process. But we should not defer in respect to whether its solution . . . insulates legislators from effective electoral challenge." *Shrink Missouri*, 528 U. S., at 403–404 (concurring opinion).

ration would do well to cultivate stable, long-term relationships of dependency.

So we do not have a solid theoretical basis for condemning §203 as a front for incumbent self-protection, and it seems equally if not more plausible that restrictions on corporate electioneering will be self-denying. Nor do we have a good empirical case for skepticism, as the Court's failure to cite any empirical research attests. Nor does the legislative history give reason for concern. Congress devoted years of careful study to the issues underlying BCRA; "[f]ew legislative proposals in recent years have received as much sustained public commentary or news coverage"; "[p]olitical scientists and academic experts . . . with no self-interest in incumbent protectio[n] were central figures in pressing the case for BCRA"; and the legislation commanded bipartisan support from the outset. Pildes, The Supreme Court 2003 Term Foreword: The Constitutionalization of Democratic Politics, 118 Harv. L. Rev. 28, 137 (2004). Finally, it is important to remember just how incumbent-friendly congressional races were prior to BCRA's passage. As the Solicitor General aptly remarked at the time, "the evidence supports overwhelmingly that incumbents were able to get re-elected under the old system just fine." Tr. of Oral Arg. in *McConnell* v. *FEC*, O. T. 2003, No. 02–1674, p. 61. "It would be hard to develop a scheme that could be better for incumbents." *Id.,* at 63.

In this case, then, "there is no convincing evidence that th[e] important interests favoring expenditure limits are fronts for incumbency protection." *Randall,* 548 U. S., at 279 (STEVENS, J., dissenting). "In the meantime, a legislative judgment that 'enough is enough' should command the greatest possible deference from judges interpreting a constitutional provision that, at best, has an indirect relationship to activity that affects the quantity . . . of repetitive speech in the marketplace of ideas." *Id.,* at 279–

280. The majority cavalierly ignores Congress' factual findings and its constitutional judgment: It acknowledges the validity of the interest in preventing corruption, but it effectively discounts the value of that interest to zero. This is quite different from conscientious policing for impermissibly anticompetitive motive or effect in a sensitive First Amendment context. It is the denial of Congress' authority to regulate corporate spending on elections.

Austin and Corporate Expenditures

Just as the majority gives short shrift to the general societal interests at stake in campaign finance regulation, it also overlooks the distinctive considerations raised by the regulation of *corporate* expenditures. The majority fails to appreciate that *Austin*'s antidistortion rationale is itself an anticorruption rationale, see 494 U. S., at 660 (describing "a different type of corruption"), tied to the special concerns raised by corporations. Understood properly, "antidistortion" is simply a variant on the classic governmental interest in protecting against improper influences on officeholders that debilitate the democratic process. It is manifestly not just an "'equalizing'" ideal in disguise. *Ante*, at 34 (quoting *Buckley*, 424 U. S., at 48).[69]

---

[69]THE CHIEF JUSTICE denies this, *ante*, at 9–10, citing scholarship that has interpreted *Austin* to endorse an equality rationale, along with an article by Justice Thurgood Marshall's former law clerk that states that Marshall, the author of *Austin*, accepted "equality of opportunity" and "equalizing access to the political process" as bases for campaign finance regulation, Garrett, New Voices in Politics: Justice Marshall's Jurisprudence on Law and Politics, 52 Howard L. J. 655, 667–668 (2009) (internal quotation marks omitted). It is fair to say that *Austin* can bear an egalitarian reading, and I have no reason to doubt this characterization of Justice Marshall's beliefs. But the fact that *Austin* can be read a certain way hardly proves THE CHIEF JUSTICE's charge that there is nothing more to it. Many of our precedents can bear multiple readings, and many of our doctrines have some "equalizing" implications but do not rest on an equalizing theory: for example, our

Opinion of STEVENS, J.

1. *Antidistortion*

The fact that corporations are different from human beings might seem to need no elaboration, except that the majority opinion almost completely elides it. *Austin* set forth some of the basic differences. Unlike natural persons, corporations have "limited liability" for their owners and managers, "perpetual life," separation of ownership and control, "and favorable treatment of the accumulation and distribution of assets . . . that enhance their ability to attract capital and to deploy their resources in ways that maximize the return on their shareholders' investments." 494 U. S., at 658–659. Unlike voters in U. S. elections, corporations may be foreign controlled.[70] Unlike other interest groups, business corporations have been "effectively delegated responsibility for ensuring society's economic welfare";[71] they inescapably structure the life of every citizen. "'[T]he resources in the treasury of a business corporation,'" furthermore, "'are not an indication of popular support for the corporation's political ideas.'" *Id.,* at 659 (quoting *MCFL*, 479 U. S., at 258). "'They reflect instead the economically motivated decisions of investors and customers. The availability of these resources may

---

takings jurisprudence and numerous rules of criminal procedure. More important, the *Austin* Court expressly declined to rely on a speech-equalization rationale, see 494 U. S., at 660, and we have never understood *Austin* to stand for such a rationale. Whatever his personal views, Justice Marshall simply did not write the opinion that THE CHIEF JUSTICE suggests he did; indeed, he "would have viewed it as irresponsible to write an opinion that boldly staked out a rationale based on equality that no one other than perhaps Justice White would have even considered joining," Garrett, 52 Howard L. J., at 674.

[70] In state elections, even domestic corporations may be "foreign"-controlled in the sense that they are incorporated in another jurisdiction and primarily owned and operated by out-of-state residents.

[71] Regan, Corporate Speech and Civic Virtue, in Debating Democracy's Discontent 289, 302 (A. Allen & M. Regan eds. 1998) (hereinafter Regan).

make a corporation a formidable political presence, even though the power of the corporation may be no reflection of the power of its ideas.'" 494 U. S., at 659 (quoting *MCFL*, 479 U. S., at 258).[72]

It might also be added that corporations have no consciences, no beliefs, no feelings, no thoughts, no desires. Corporations help structure and facilitate the activities of human beings, to be sure, and their "personhood" often serves as a useful legal fiction. But they are not themselves members of "We the People" by whom and for whom our Constitution was established.

These basic points help explain why corporate electioneering is not only more likely to impair compelling governmental interests, but also why restrictions on that electioneering are less likely to encroach upon First Amendment freedoms. One fundamental concern of the First Amendment is to "protec[t] the individual's interest in self-expression." *Consolidated Edison Co. of N. Y.* v. *Public Serv. Comm'n of N. Y.*, 447 U. S. 530, 534, n. 2 (1980); see also *Bellotti*, 435 U. S., at 777, n. 12. Freedom of speech helps "make men free to develop their faculties," *Whitney* v. *California*, 274 U. S. 357, 375 (1927) (Brandeis,

---

[72] Nothing in this analysis turns on whether the corporation is conceptualized as a grantee of a state concession, see, *e.g., Trustees of Dartmouth College* v. *Woodward*, 4 Wheat. 518, 636 (1819) (Marshall, C. J.), a nexus of explicit and implicit contracts, see, *e.g.,* F. Easterbrook & D. Fischel, The Economic Structure of Corporate Law 12 (1991), a mediated hierarchy of stakeholders, see, *e.g.,* Blair & Stout, A Team Production Theory of Corporate Law, 85 Va. L. Rev. 247 (1999) (hereinafter Blair & Stout), or any other recognized model. *Austin* referred to the structure and the advantages of corporations as "state-conferred" in several places, 494 U. S., at 660, 665, 667, but its antidistortion argument relied only on the basic descriptive features of corporations, as sketched above. It is not necessary to agree on a precise theory of the corporation to agree that corporations differ from natural persons in fundamental ways, and that a legislature might therefore need to regulate them differently if it is human welfare that is the object of its concern. Cf. Hansmann & Kraakman 441, n. 5.

J., concurring), it respects their "dignity and choice," *Cohen* v. *California*, 403 U. S. 15, 24 (1971), and it facilitates the value of "individual self-realization," Redish, The Value of Free Speech, 130 U. Pa. L. Rev. 591, 594 (1982). Corporate speech, however, is derivative speech, speech by proxy. A regulation such as BCRA §203 may affect the way in which individuals disseminate certain messages through the corporate form, but it does not prevent anyone from speaking in his or her own voice. "Within the realm of [campaign spending] generally," corporate spending is "furthest from the core of political expression." *Beaumont*, 539 U. S., at 161, n. 8.

It is an interesting question "who" is even speaking when a business corporation places an advertisement that endorses or attacks a particular candidate. Presumably it is not the customers or employees, who typically have no say in such matters. It cannot realistically be said to be the shareholders, who tend to be far removed from the day-to-day decisions of the firm and whose political preferences may be opaque to management. Perhaps the officers or directors of the corporation have the best claim to be the ones speaking, except their fiduciary duties generally prohibit them from using corporate funds for personal ends. Some individuals associated with the corporation must make the decision to place the ad, but the idea that these individuals are thereby fostering their self-expression or cultivating their critical faculties is fanciful. It is entirely possible that the corporation's electoral message will *conflict* with their personal convictions. Take away the ability to use general treasury funds for some of those ads, and no one's autonomy, dignity, or political equality has been impinged upon in the least.

Corporate expenditures are distinguishable from individual expenditures in this respect. I have taken the view that a legislature may place reasonable restrictions on individuals' electioneering expenditures in the service of the governmental interests explained above, and in recognition of the fact that such restrictions are not direct restraints on speech but rather on its financing. See, *e.g., Randall,* 548 U. S., at 273 (dissenting opinion). But those restrictions concededly present a tougher case, because the primary conduct of actual, flesh-and-blood persons is involved. Some of those individuals might feel that they need to spend large sums of money on behalf of a particular candidate to vindicate the intensity of their electoral preferences. This is obviously not the situation with business corporations, as their routine practice of giving "substantial sums to *both* major national parties" makes pellucidly clear. *McConnell,* 540 U. S., at 148. "[C]orporate participation" in elections, any business executive will tell you, "is more transactional than ideological." Supp. Brief for Committee for Economic Development as *Amicus Curiae* 10.

In this transactional spirit, some corporations have affirmatively urged Congress to place limits on their electioneering communications. These corporations fear that officeholders will shake them down for supportive ads, that they will have to spend increasing sums on elections in an ever-escalating arms race with their competitors, and that public trust in business will be eroded. See *id.,* at 10–19. A system that effectively forces corporations to use their shareholders' money both to maintain access to, and to avoid retribution from, elected officials may ultimately prove more harmful than beneficial to many corporations. It can impose a kind of implicit tax.[73]

---

[73] Not all corporations support BCRA §203, of course, and not all corporations are large business entities or their tax-exempt adjuncts. Some nonprofit corporations are created for an ideological purpose. Some closely held corporations are strongly identified with a particular owner or founder. The fact that §203, like the statute at issue in *Austin,* regulates some of these corporations' expenditures does not disturb the analysis above. See 494 U. S., at 661–665. Small-business

In short, regulations such as §203 and the statute upheld in *Austin* impose only a limited burden on First
Amendment freedoms not only because they target a
narrow subset of expenditures and leave untouched the
broader "public dialogue," *ante*, at 25, but also because
they leave untouched the speech of natural persons.
Recognizing the weakness of a speaker-based critique of
Austin, the Court places primary emphasis not on the
corporation's right to electioneer, but rather on the listener's interest in hearing what every possible speaker
may have to say. The Court's central argument is that
laws such as §203 have "'deprived [the electorate] of information, knowledge and opinion vital to its function,'"
ante, at 38 (quoting *CIO*, 335 U. S., at 144 (Rutledge, J.,
concurring in judgment)), and this, in turn, "interferes
with the 'open marketplace' of ideas protected by the First
Amendment," *ante*, at 38 (quoting *New York State Bd. of
Elections* v. *Lopez Torres*, 552 U. S. 196, 208 (2008)).

There are many flaws in this argument. If the overrid-
ing concern depends on the interests of the audience,
surely the public's perception of the value of corporate
speech should be given important weight. That perception
today is the same as it was a century ago when Theodore
Roosevelt delivered the speeches to Congress that, in time,
led to the limited prohibition on corporate campaign expenditures that is overruled today. See *WRTL*, 551 U. S.,
at 509–510 (Souter, J., dissenting) (summarizing President

---

owners may speak in their own names, rather than the business', if
they wish to evade §203 altogether. Nonprofit corporations that want
to make unrestricted electioneering expenditures may do so if they
refuse donations from businesses and unions and permit members to
disassociate without economic penalty. See *MCFL*, 479 U. S. 238, 264
(1986). Making it plain that their decision is not motivated by a concern about BCRA's coverage of nonprofits that have ideological mis-
sions but lack *MCFL* status, our colleagues refuse to apply the Snowe-
Jeffords Amendment or the lower courts' *de minimis* exception to
MCFL. See *ante*, at 10–12.

Roosevelt's remarks). The distinctive threat to democratic integrity posed by corporate domination of politics was recognized at "the inception of the republic" and "has been a persistent theme in American political life" ever since. Regan 302. It is only certain Members of this Court, not the listeners themselves, who have agitated for more corporate electioneering.

Austin recognized that there are substantial reasons why a legislature might conclude that unregulated general treasury expenditures will give corporations "unfai[r] influence" in the electoral process, 494 U. S., at 660, and distort public debate in ways that undermine rather than advance the interests of listeners. The legal structure of corporations allows them to amass and deploy financial resources on a scale few natural persons can match. The structure of a business corporation, furthermore, draws a line between the corporation's economic interests and the political preferences of the individuals associated with the corporation; the corporation must engage the electoral process with the aim "to enhance the profitability of the company, no matter how persuasive the arguments for a broader or conflicting set of priorities," Brief for American Independent Business Alliance as *Amicus Curiae* 11; see also ALI, Principles of Corporate Governance: Analysis and Recommendations §2.01(a), p. 55 (1992) ("[A] corporation . . . should have as its objective the conduct of business activities with a view to enhancing corporate profit and shareholder gain"). In a state election such as the one at issue in *Austin*, the interests of nonresident corporations may be fundamentally adverse to the interests of local voters. Consequently, when corporations grab up the prime broadcasting slots on the eve of an election, they can flood the market with advocacy that bears "little or no correlation" to the ideas of natural persons or to any broader notion of the public good, 494 U. S., at 660. The opinions of real people may be marginalized. "The expen-

diture restrictions of [2 U. S. C.] §441b are thus meant to
ensure that competition among actors in the political
arena is truly competition among ideas." *MCFL*, 479
U. S., at 259.

In addition to this immediate drowning out of noncorpo-
rate voices, there may be deleterious effects that follow
soon thereafter. Corporate "domination" of electioneering,
Austin, 494 U. S., at 659, can generate the impression that
corporations dominate our democracy. When citizens turn
on their televisions and radios before an election and hear
only corporate electioneering, they may lose faith in their
capacity, as citizens, to influence public policy. A Government captured by corporate interests, they may come
to believe, will be neither responsive to their needs nor
willing to give their views a fair hearing. The predictable
result is cynicism and disenchantment: an increased
perception that large spenders "'call the tune'" and a
reduced "'willingness of voters to take part in democratic
governance.'" *McConnell*, 540 U. S., at 144 (quoting
Shrink Missouri, 528 U. S., at 390). To the extent that
corporations are allowed to exert undue influence in electoral races, the speech of the eventual winners of those
races may also be chilled. Politicians who fear that a
certain corporation can make or break their reelection
chances may be cowed into silence about that corporation.
On a variety of levels, unregulated corporate electioneering might diminish the ability of citizens to "hold officials
accountable to the people," *ante*, at 23, and disserve the
goal of a public debate that is "uninhibited, robust, and
wide-open," *New York Times Co.* v. *Sullivan*, 376 U. S.
254, 270 (1964). At the least, I stress again, a legislature
is entitled to credit these concerns and to take tailored
measures in response.

The majority's unwillingness to distinguish between
corporations and humans similarly blinds it to the possibility that corporations' "war chests" and their special

"advantages" in the legal realm, *Austin,* 494 U. S., at 659, may translate into special advantages in the market for legislation. When large numbers of citizens have a common stake in a measure that is under consideration, it may be very difficult for them to coordinate resources on behalf of their position. The corporate form, by contrast, "provides a simple way to channel rents to only those who have paid their dues, as it were. If you do not own stock, you do not benefit from the larger dividends or appreciation in the stock price caused by the passage of private interest legislation." Sitkoff, Corporate Political Speech, Political Extortion, and the Competition for Corporate Charters, 69 U. Chi. L. Rev. 1103, 1113 (2002). Corporations, that is, are uniquely equipped to seek laws that favor their owners, not simply because they have a lot of money but because of their legal and organizational structure. Remove all restrictions on their electioneering, and the door may be opened to a type of rent seeking that is "far more destructive" than what noncorporations are capable of. *Ibid.* It is for reasons such as these that our campaign finance jurisprudence has long appreciated that "the 'differing structures and purposes' of different entities 'may require different forms of regulation in order to protect the integrity of the electoral process.'" *NRWC,* 459 U. S., at 210 (quoting *California Medical Assn.,* 453 U. S., at 201).

The Court's facile depiction of corporate electioneering assumes away all of these complexities. Our colleagues ridicule the idea of regulating expenditures based on "nothing more" than a fear that corporations have a special "ability to persuade," *ante,* at 11 (opinion of ROBERTS, C. J.), as if corporations were our society's ablest debaters and viewpoint-neutral laws such as §203 were created to suppress their best arguments. In their haste to knock down yet another straw man, our colleagues simply ignore the fundamental concerns of the *Austin* Court and the

legislatures that have passed laws like §203: to safeguard
the integrity, competitiveness, and democratic responsiveness of the electoral process. All of the majority's theoretical arguments turn on a proposition with undeniable
surface appeal but little grounding in evidence or experience, "that there is no such thing as too much speech,"
Austin, 494 U. S., at 695 (SCALIA, J., dissenting)).[74] If
individuals in our society had infinite free time to listen to
and contemplate every last bit of speech uttered by anyone, anywhere; and if broadcast advertisements had no
special ability to influence elections apart from the merits
of their arguments (to the extent they make any); and if
legislators always operated with nothing less than perfect
virtue; then I suppose the majority's premise would be
sound. In the real world, we have seen, corporate domination of the airwaves prior to an election may decrease the
average listener's exposure to relevant viewpoints, and it
may diminish citizens' willingness and capacity to participate in the democratic process.

None of this is to suggest that corporations can or
should be denied an opportunity to participate in election
campaigns or in any other public forum (much less that a
work of art such as *Mr. Smith Goes to Washington* may be
banned), or to deny that some corporate speech may contribute significantly to public debate. What it shows,
however, is that *Austin*'s "concern about corporate domination of the political process," 494 U. S., at 659, reflects
more than a concern to protect governmental interests
outside of the First Amendment. It also reflects a concern
to *facilitate* First Amendment values by preserving some
breathing room around the electoral "marketplace" of
ideas, *ante*, at 19, 34, 38, 52, 54, the marketplace in which
the actual people of this Nation determine how they will

---

[74] Of course, no presiding person in a courtroom, legislature, class-
room, polling place, or family dinner would take this hyperbole literally.

govern themselves. The majority seems oblivious to the simple truth that laws such as §203 do not merely pit the anticorruption interest against the First Amendment, but also pit competing First Amendment values against each other. There are, to be sure, serious concerns with any effort to balance the First Amendment rights of speakers against the First Amendment rights of listeners. But when the speakers in question are not real people and when the appeal to "First Amendment principles" depends almost entirely on the listeners' perspective, *ante,* at 1, 48, it becomes necessary to consider how listeners will actually be affected.

In critiquing *Austin's* antidistortion rationale and campaign finance regulation more generally, our colleagues place tremendous weight on the example of media corporations. See *ante,* at 35–38, 46; *ante,* at 1, 11 (opinion of ROBERTS, C. J.); *ante,* at 6 (opinion of SCALIA, J.). Yet it is not at all clear that *Austin* would permit §203 to be applied to them. The press plays a unique role not only in the text, history, and structure of the First Amendment but also in facilitating public discourse; as the *Austin* Court explained, "media corporations differ significantly from other corporations in that their resources are devoted to the collection of information and its dissemination to the public," 494 U. S., at 667. Our colleagues have raised some interesting and difficult questions about Congress' authority to regulate electioneering by the press, and about how to define what constitutes the press. *But that is not the case before us.* Section 203 does not apply to media corporations, and even if it did, Citizens United is not a media corporation. There would be absolutely no reason to consider the issue of media corporations if the majority did not, first, transform Citizens United's as-applied challenge into a facial challenge and, second, invent the theory that legislatures must eschew all "identity"-based distinctions and treat a local nonprofit news outlet exactly the same as General Motors.[75] This calls to mind George Berkeley's description of philosophers: "[W]e have first raised a dust and then complain we cannot see." Principles of Human Knowledge/Three Dialogues 38, ¶3 (R. Woolhouse ed. 1988).

It would be perfectly understandable if our colleagues feared that a campaign finance regulation such as §203 may be counterproductive or self-interested, and therefore attended carefully to the choices the Legislature has made. But the majority does not bother to consider such practical matters, or even to consult a record; it simply stipulates that "enlightened self-government" can arise only in the absence of regulation. *Ante*, at 23. In light of the distinctive features of corporations identified in *Austin*, there is no valid basis for this assumption. The marketplace of ideas is not actually a place where items—or laws—are meant to be bought and sold, and when we move from the realm of economics to the realm of corporate electioneering, there may be no "reason to think the market ordering is intrinsically good at all," Strauss 1386.

The Court's blinkered and aphoristic approach to the First Amendment may well promote corporate power at the cost of the individual and collective self-expression the Amendment was meant to serve. It will undoubtedly cripple the ability of ordinary citizens, Congress, and the States to adopt even limited measures to protect against corporate domination of the electoral process. Americans may be forgiven if they do not feel the Court has advanced

---

[75] Under the majority's view, the legislature is thus damned if it does and damned if it doesn't. If the legislature gives media corporations an exemption from electioneering regulations that apply to other corporations, it violates the newly minted First Amendment rule against identity-based distinctions. If the legislature does not give media corporations an exemption, it violates the First Amendment rights of the press. The only way out of this invented bind: no regulations whatsoever.

the cause of self-government today.

2. *Shareholder Protection*

There is yet another way in which laws such as §203 can serve First Amendment values. Interwoven with *Austin*'s concern to protect the integrity of the electoral process is a concern to protect the rights of shareholders from a kind of coerced speech: electioneering expenditures that do not "reflec[t] [their] support." 494 U. S., at 660–661. When corporations use general treasury funds to praise or attack a particular candidate for office, it is the shareholders, as the residual claimants, who are effectively footing the bill. Those shareholders who disagree with the corporation's electoral message may find their financial investments being used to undermine their political convictions.

The PAC mechanism, by contrast, helps assure that those who pay for an electioneering communication actually support its content and that managers do not use general treasuries to advance personal agendas. *Ibid.* It "'allows corporate political participation without the temptation to use corporate funds for political influence, quite possibly at odds with the sentiments of some shareholders or members.'" *McConnell*, 540 U. S., at 204 (quoting *Beaumont*, 539 U. S., at 163). A rule that privileges the use of PACs thus does more than facilitate the political speech of like-minded shareholders; it also curbs the rent seeking behavior of executives and respects the views of dissenters. *Austin*'s acceptance of restrictions on general treasury spending "simply allows people who have invested in the business corporation for purely economic reasons"—the vast majority of investors, one assumes—"to avoid being taken advantage of, without sacrificing their economic objectives." Winkler, Beyond *Bellotti*, 32 Loyola (LA) L. Rev. 133, 201 (1998).

The concern to protect dissenting shareholders and union members has a long history in campaign finance reform. It provided a central motivation for the Tillman Act in 1907 and subsequent legislation, see *Pipefitters* v. *United States*, 407 U. S. 385, 414–415 (1972); Winkler, 92 Geo. L. J., at 887–900, and it has been endorsed in a long line of our cases, see, *e.g., McConnell*, 540 U. S., at 204–205; *Beaumont*, 539 U. S., at 152–154; *MCFL*, 479 U. S., at 258; *NRWC*, 459 U. S., at 207–208; *Pipefitters*, 407 U. S., at 414–416; see also n. 60, *supra*. Indeed, we have unanimously recognized the governmental interest in "protect[ing] the individuals who have paid money into a corporation or union for purposes other than the support of candidates from having that money used to support political candidates to whom they may be opposed." *NRWC*, 459 U. S., at 207–208.

The Court dismisses this interest on the ground that abuses of shareholder money can be corrected "through the procedures of corporate democracy," *ante*, at 46 (internal quotation marks omitted), and, it seems, through Internet-based disclosures, *ante*, at 55.[76] I fail to understand how this addresses the concerns of dissenting union members, who will also be affected by today's ruling, and I fail to understand why the Court is so confident in these mechanisms. By "corporate democracy," presumably the Court means the rights of shareholders to vote and to bring derivative suits for breach of fiduciary duty. In practice, however, many corporate lawyers will tell you that "these rights are so limited as to be almost nonexis-

---

[76] I note that, among the many other regulatory possibilities it has left open, ranging from new versions of §203 supported by additional evidence of *quid pro quo* corruption or its appearance to any number of tax incentive or public financing schemes, today's decision does not require that a legislature rely solely on these mechanisms to protect shareholders. Legislatures remain free in their incorporation and tax laws to condition the types of activity in which corporations may engage, including electioneering activity, on specific disclosure requirements or on prior express approval by shareholders or members.

tent," given the internal authority wielded by boards and managers and the expansive protections afforded by the business judgment rule. Blair & Stout 320; see also *id.,* at 298–315; Winkler, 32 Loyola (LA) L. Rev., at 165–166, 199–200. Modern technology may help make it easier to track corporate activity, including electoral advocacy, but it is utopian to believe that it solves the problem. Most American households that own stock do so through intermediaries such as mutual funds and pension plans, see Evans, A Requiem for the Retail Investor? 95 Va. L. Rev. 1105 (2009), which makes it more difficult both to monitor and to alter particular holdings. Studies show that a majority of individual investors make no trades at all during a given year. *Id.,* at 1117. Moreover, if the corporation in question operates a PAC, an investor who sees the company's ads may not know whether they are being funded through the PAC or through the general treasury.

If and when shareholders learn that a corporation has been spending general treasury money on objectionable electioneering, they can divest. Even assuming that they reliably learn as much, however, this solution is only partial. The injury to the shareholders' expressive rights has already occurred; they might have preferred to keep that corporation's stock in their portfolio for any number of economic reasons; and they may incur a capital gains tax or other penalty from selling their shares, changing their pension plan, or the like. The shareholder protection rationale has been criticized as underinclusive, in that corporations also spend money on lobbying and charitable contributions in ways that any particular shareholder might disapprove. But those expenditures do not implicate the selection of public officials, an area in which "the interests of unwilling . . . corporate shareholders [in not being] forced to subsidize that speech" "are at their zenith." *Austin,* 494 U. S., at 677 (Brennan, J., concurring). And in any event, the question is whether shareholder protection provides a basis for regulating expenditures in the weeks before an election, not whether additional types of corporate communications might similarly be conditioned on voluntariness.

Recognizing the limits of the shareholder protection rationale, the *Austin* Court did not hold it out as an adequate and independent ground for sustaining the statute in question. Rather, the Court applied it to reinforce the antidistortion rationale, in two main ways. First, the problem of dissenting shareholders shows that even if electioneering expenditures can advance the political views of some members of a corporation, they will often compromise the views of others. See, *e.g., id.,* at 663 (discussing risk that corporation's "members may be . . . reluctant to withdraw as members even if they disagree with [its] political expression"). Second, it provides an additional reason, beyond the distinctive legal attributes of the corporate form, for doubting that these "expenditures reflect actual public support for the political ideas espoused," *id.,* at 660. The shareholder protection rationale, in other words, bolsters the conclusion that restrictions on corporate electioneering can serve both speakers' and listeners' interests, as well as the anticorruption interest. And it supplies yet another reason why corporate expenditures merit less protection than individual expenditures.

V

Today's decision is backwards in many senses. It elevates the majority's agenda over the litigants' submissions, facial attacks over as-applied claims, broad constitutional theories over narrow statutory grounds, individual dissenting opinions over precedential holdings, assertion over tradition, absolutism over empiricism, rhetoric over reality. Our colleagues have arrived at the conclusion that *Austin* must be overruled and that §203 is facially unconstitutional only after mischaracterizing both the reach and rationale of those authorities, and after bypassing or ignoring rules of judicial restraint used to cabin the Court's lawmaking power. Their conclusion that the societal interest in avoiding corruption and the appearance of corruption does not provide an adequate justification for regulating corporate expenditures on candidate elections relies on an incorrect description of that interest, along with a failure to acknowledge the relevance of established facts and the considered judgments of state and federal legislatures over many decades.

In a democratic society, the longstanding consensus on the need to limit corporate campaign spending should outweigh the wooden application of judge-made rules. The majority's rejection of this principle "elevate[s] corporations to a level of deference which has not been seen at least since the days when substantive due process was regularly used to invalidate regulatory legislation thought to unfairly impinge upon established economic interests." *Bellotti*, 435 U. S., at 817, n. 13 (White, J., dissenting). At bottom, the Court's opinion is thus a rejection of the common sense of the American people, who have recognized a need to prevent corporations from undermining self-government since the founding, and who have fought against the distinctive corrupting potential of corporate electioneering since the days of Theodore Roosevelt. It is a strange time to repudiate that common sense. While American democracy is imperfect, few outside the majority of this Court would have thought its flaws included a dearth of corporate money in politics.

I would affirm the judgment of the District Court.

SUPREME COURT OF THE UNITED STATES

No. 08–205

CITIZENS UNITED, APPELLANT *v.* FEDERAL
ELECTION COMMISSION

ON APPEAL FROM THE UNITED STATES DISTRICT COURT FOR
THE DISTRICT OF COLUMBIA

[January 21, 2010]

JUSTICE THOMAS, concurring in part and dissenting in part.

I join all but Part IV of the Court's opinion.

Political speech is entitled to robust protection under the First Amendment. Section 203 of the Bipartisan Campaign Reform Act of 2002 (BCRA) has never been reconcilable with that protection. By striking down §203, the Court takes an important first step toward restoring full constitutional protection to speech that is "indispensable to the effective and intelligent use of the processes of popular government." *McConnell* v. *Federal Election Comm'n*, 540 U. S. 93, 265 (2003) (THOMAS, J., concurring in part, concurring in judgment in part, and dissenting in part) (internal quotation marks omitted). I dissent from Part IV of the Court's opinion, however, because the Court's constitutional analysis does not go far enough. The disclosure, disclaimer, and reporting requirements in BCRA §§201 and 311 are also unconstitutional. See *id.,* at 275–277, and n. 10.

Congress may not abridge the "right to anonymous speech" based on the "'simple interest in providing voters with additional relevant information,'" *id.,* at 276 (quoting *McIntyre* v. *Ohio Elections Comm'n*, 514 U. S. 334, 348 (1995)). In continuing to hold otherwise, the Court misapprehends the import of "recent events" that some *amici* describe "in which donors to certain causes were black-listed, threatened, or otherwise targeted for retaliation." *Ante,* at 54. The Court properly recognizes these events as "cause for concern," *ibid.,* but fails to acknowledge their constitutional significance. In my view, *amici*'s submissions show why the Court's insistence on upholding §§201 and 311 will ultimately prove as misguided (and ill fated) as was its prior approval of §203.

Amici's examples relate principally to Proposition 8, a state ballot proposition that California voters narrowly passed in the 2008 general election. Proposition 8 amended California's constitution to provide that "[o]nly marriage between a man and a woman is valid or recognized in California." Cal. Const., Art. I, §7.5. Any donor who gave more than $100 to any committee supporting or opposing Proposition 8 was required to disclose his full name, street address, occupation, employer's name (or business name, if self-employed), and the total amount of his contributions.[1] See Cal. Govt. Code Ann. §84211(f) (West 2005). The California Secretary of State was then required to post this information on the Internet. See §§84600–84601; §§84602–84602.1 (West Supp. 2010); §§84602.5–84604 (West 2005); §85605 (West Supp. 2010); §§84606–84609 (West 2005).

Some opponents of Proposition 8 compiled this information and created Web sites with maps showing the locations of homes or businesses of Proposition 8 supporters. Many supporters (or their customers) suffered property damage, or threats of physical violence or death, as a

---

[1] BCRA imposes similar disclosure requirements. See, *e.g.,* 2 U. S. C. §434(f)(2)(F) ("Every person who makes a disbursement for the direct costs of producing and airing electioneering communications in an aggregate amount in excess of $10,000 during any calendar year" must disclose "the names and addresses of all contributors who contributed an aggregate amount of $1,000 or more to the person making the disbursement").

result. They cited these incidents in a complaint they filed after the 2008 election, seeking to invalidate California's mandatory disclosure laws. Supporters recounted being told: "Consider yourself lucky. If I had a gun I would have gunned you down along with each and every other supporter," or, "we have plans for you and your friends." Complaint in *ProtectMarriage.com—Yes on 8* v. *Bowen*, Case No. 2:09–cv–00058–MCE–DAD (ED Cal.), ¶31. Proposition 8 opponents also allegedly harassed the measure's supporters by defacing or damaging their property. *Id.,* ¶32. Two religious organizations supporting Proposition 8 reportedly received through the mail envelopes containing a white powdery substance. *Id.,* ¶33.

Those accounts are consistent with media reports describing Proposition 8-related retaliation. The director of the nonprofit California Musical Theater gave $1,000 to support the initiative; he was forced to resign after artists complained to his employer. Lott & Smith, Donor Disclosure Has Its Downsides, Wall Street Journal, Dec. 26, 2008, p. A13. The director of the Los Angeles Film Festival was forced to resign after giving $1,500 because opponents threatened to boycott and picket the next festival. *Ibid.* And a woman who had managed her popular, family-owned restaurant for 26 years was forced to resign after she gave $100, because "throngs of [angry] protesters" repeatedly arrived at the restaurant and "shout[ed] 'shame on you' at customers." Lopez, Prop. 8 Stance Upends Her Life, Los Angeles Times, Dec. 14, 2008, p. B1. The police even had to "arriv[e] in riot gear one night to quell the angry mob" at the restaurant. *Ibid.* Some supporters of Proposition 8 engaged in similar tactics; one real estate businessman in San Diego who had donated to a group opposing Proposition 8 "received a letter from the Prop. 8 Executive Committee threatening to publish his company's name if he didn't also donate to the 'Yes on 8' campaign." Donor Disclosure, *supra,* at A13.

The success of such intimidation tactics has apparently spawned a cottage industry that uses forcibly disclosed donor information to *pre-empt* citizens' exercise of their First Amendment rights. Before the 2008 Presidential election, a "newly formed nonprofit group . . . plann[ed] to confront donors to conservative groups, hoping to create a chilling effect that will dry up contributions." Luo, Group Plans Campaign Against G.O.P. Donors, N. Y. Times, Aug. 8, 2008, p. A15. Its leader, "who described his effort as 'going for the jugular,'" detailed the group's plan to send a "warning letter . . . alerting donors who might be considering giving to right-wing groups to a variety of potential dangers, including legal trouble, public exposure and watchdog groups digging through their lives." *Ibid.*

These instances of retaliation sufficiently demonstrate why this Court should invalidate mandatory disclosure and reporting requirements. But *amici* present evidence of yet another reason to do so—the threat of retaliation from *elected officials*. As *amici*'s submissions make clear, this threat extends far beyond a single ballot proposition in California. For example, a candidate challenging an incumbent state attorney general reported that some members of the State's business community feared donating to his campaign because they did not want to cross the incumbent; in his words, "'I go to so many people and hear the same thing: "I sure hope you beat [the incumbent], but I can't afford to have my name on your records. He might come after me next."'" Strassel, Challenging Spitzerism at the Polls, Wall Street Journal, Aug. 1, 2008, p. A11. The incumbent won reelection in 2008.

My point is not to express any view on the merits of the political controversies I describe. Rather, it is to demonstrate—using real-world, recent examples—the fallacy in the Court's conclusion that "[d]isclaimer and disclosure requirements . . . impose no ceiling on campaign-related activities, and do not prevent anyone from speaking."

Ante, at 51 (internal quotation marks and citations omitted). Of course they do. Disclaimer and disclosure requirements enable private citizens and elected officials to implement political strategies *specifically calculated* to curtail campaign-related activity and prevent the lawful, peaceful exercise of First Amendment rights.

The Court nevertheless insists that as-applied challenges to disclosure requirements will suffice to vindicate those speech rights, as long as potential plaintiffs can "show a reasonable probability that disclosure . . . will subject them to threats, harassment, or reprisals from either Government officials or private parties." *Ante*, at 52 (internal quotation marks omitted). But the Court's opinion itself proves the irony in this compromise. In correctly explaining why it must address the facial constitutionality of §203, see *ante*, at 5–20, the Court recognizes that "[t]he First Amendment does not permit laws that force speakers to . . . seek declaratory rulings before discussing the most salient political issues of our day," *ante*, at 7; that as-applied challenges to §203 "would require substantial litigation over an extended time" and result in an "interpretive process [that] itself would create an inevitable, pervasive, and serious risk of chilling protected speech pending the drawing of fine distinctions that, in the end, would themselves be questionable," *ante*, at 9–10; that "a court would be remiss in performing its duties were it to accept an unsound principle merely to avoid the necessity of making a broader ruling," *ante*, at 12; and that avoiding a facial challenge to §203 "would prolong the substantial, nation-wide chilling effect" that §203 causes, *ante*, at 16. This logic, of course, applies equally to as-applied challenges to §§201 and 311.

Irony aside, the Court's promise that as-applied challenges will adequately protect speech is a hollow assurance. Now more than ever, §§201 and 311 will chill protected speech because—as California voters can attest—

"the advent of the Internet" enables "prompt disclosure of expenditures," which "provide[s]" political opponents "with the information needed" to intimidate and retaliate against their foes. *Ante*, at 55. Thus, "disclosure permits citizens . . . to react to the speech of [their political opponents] in a proper"—or undeniably *improper*—"way" long before a plaintiff could prevail on an as-applied challenge.[2] *Ibid.*

I cannot endorse a view of the First Amendment that subjects citizens of this Nation to death threats, ruined careers, damaged or defaced property, or pre-emptive and threatening warning letters as the price for engaging in "core political speech, the 'primary object of First Amendment protection.'" *McConnell*, 540 U. S., at 264 (THOMAS, J., concurring in part, concurring in judgment in part, and dissenting in part) (quoting *Nixon* v. *Shrink Missouri Government PAC*, 528 U. S. 377, 410–411 (2000) (THOMAS, J., dissenting)). Accordingly, I respectfully dissent from the Court's judgment upholding BCRA §§201 and 311.

---

[2] But cf. *Hill* v. *Colorado*, 530 U. S. 703, 707–710 (2000) (approving a statute restricting speech "within 100 feet" of abortion clinics because it protected women seeking an abortion from "'sidewalk counseling,'" which "consists of efforts 'to educate, counsel, persuade, or inform passersby about abortion and abortion alternatives by means of verbal or written speech,'" and which "sometimes" involved "strong and abusive language in face-to-face encounters").